The Tragedie of
Othello
The Moore of Venice

By Edward de Vere

Art:
Portrait of Edward de Vere
17th Earl of Oxford (1550-1604)

This edition produced by
Verus Publishing

V | P

www.verusbooks.com

ISBN: 978-1-951267-36-0
Imprint / Publisher: Verus Publishing

The Author

Edward de Vere, 17th Earl of Oxford

Biography and Bibliography
After the Play

A Preverse

Drone on ye learned scholars of the day
As to with whom the words ahead the credit lay.
For our part though can be no further doubt
That the author of these words has been found out
To be a person lordly and refined
On whom the light of wit so boldly shined
That to keep this wit from tearing in the fray
He gave another, lesser wit his say.

Now let the least of wits
That writes these paltry lines
Yield to him whose peerless name
Should be with reverence spake.
Let this name be not of history's misassigns
Whose pen and verse have made the earth to shake.

The Tragedie of
Othello
The Moore of Venice

By Edward de Vere

The Main Characters

Othello – General in the Venetian army.

Desdemona – Othello's wife and daughter of Brabantio.

Iago – Othello's trusted ensign.

Cassio – Othello's loyal captain.

Bianca – Cassio's lover

Emilia – Iago's wife and Desdemona's maidservant.

Brabantio – Venetian senator and Desdemona's father

Roderigo – A dissolute Venetian who is in love with Desdemona.

Doge of Venice

Gratiano – Brabantio's brother.

Lodovico – Brabantio's kinsman & relative of Desdemona.

Montano – Othello's Venetian predecessor in the government of Cyprus.

Clown

Senators

Sailor

And now, the Play...

ACT I

SCENE I.

Venice. A street.

Enter RODERIGO and IAGO

RODERIGO
    Tush! never tell me; I take it much unkindly
    That thou, Iago, who hast had my purse
    As if the strings were thine, shouldst know of this.
IAGO
    'Sblood, but you will not hear me:
    If ever I did dream of such a matter, Abhor me.
RODERIGO
    Thou told'st me thou didst hold him in thy hate.
IAGO
    Despise me, if I do not. Three great ones of the city,
    In personal suit to make me his lieutenant,
    Off-capp'd to him: and, by the faith of man,
    I know my price, I am worth no worse a place:
    But he; as loving his own pride and purposes,
    Evades them, with a bombast circumstance
    Horribly stuff'd with epithets of war;
    And, in conclusion,
    Nonsuits my mediators; for, 'Certes,' says he,
    'I have already chose my officer.'
    And what was he?
    Forsooth, a great arithmetician,
    One Michael Cassio, a Florentine,
    A fellow almost damn'd in a fair wife;
    That never set a squadron in the field,
    Nor the division of a battle knows
    More than a spinster; unless the bookish theoric,

Wherein the toged consuls can propose
As masterly as he: mere prattle, without practise,
Is all his soldiership. But he, sir, had the election:
And I, of whom his eyes had seen the proof
At Rhodes, at Cyprus and on other grounds
Christian and heathen, must be be-lee'd and calm'd
By debitor and creditor: this counter-caster,
He, in good time, must his lieutenant be,
And I--God bless the mark!--his Moorship's ancient.

RODERIGO

By heaven, I rather would have been his hangman.

IAGO

Why, there's no remedy; 'tis the curse of service,
Preferment goes by letter and affection,
And not by old gradation, where each second
Stood heir to the first. Now, sir, be judge yourself,
Whether I in any just term am affined
To love the Moor.

RODERIGO

I would not follow him then.

IAGO

O, sir, content you;
I follow him to serve my turn upon him:
We cannot all be masters, nor all masters
Cannot be truly follow'd. You shall mark
Many a duteous and knee-crooking knave,
That, doting on his own obsequious bondage,
Wears out his time, much like his master's ass,
For nought but provender, and when he's old, cashier'd:
Whip me such honest knaves. Others there are
Who, trimm'd in forms and visages of duty,
Keep yet their hearts attending on themselves,
And, throwing but shows of service on their lords,
Do well thrive by them and when they have lined

their coats
Do themselves homage: these fellows have some soul;
And such a one do I profess myself. For, sir,
It is as sure as you are Roderigo,
Were I the Moor, I would not be Iago:
In following him, I follow but myself;
Heaven is my judge, not I for love and duty,
But seeming so, for my peculiar end:
For when my outward action doth demonstrate
The native act and figure of my heart
In compliment extern, 'tis not long after
But I will wear my heart upon my sleeve
For daws to peck at: I am not what I am.

RODERIGO
What a full fortune does the thicklips owe
If he can carry't thus!

IAGO
Call up her father,
Rouse him: make after him, poison his delight,
Proclaim him in the streets; incense her kinsmen,
And, though he in a fertile climate dwell,
Plague him with flies: though that his joy be joy,
Yet throw such changes of vexation on't,
As it may lose some colour.

RODERIGO
Here is her father's house; I'll call aloud.

IAGO
Do, with like timorous accent and dire yell
As when, by night and negligence, the fire
Is spied in populous cities.

RODERIGO
What, ho, Brabantio! Signior Brabantio, ho!

IAGO
Awake! what, ho, Brabantio! thieves! thieves! thieves!

Look to your house, your daughter and your bags!
Thieves! thieves!

BRABANTIO appears above, at a window

BRABANTIO
   What is the reason of this terrible summons?
   What is the matter there?
RODERIGO
   Signior, is all your family within?
IAGO
   Are your doors lock'd?
BRABANTIO
   Why, wherefore ask you this?
IAGO
   'Zounds, sir, you're robb'd; for shame, put on
   your gown;
   Your heart is burst, you have lost half your soul;
   Even now, now, very now, an old black ram
   Is topping your white ewe. Arise, arise;
   Awake the snorting citizens with the bell,
   Or else the devil will make a grandsire of you:
   Arise, I say.
BRABANTIO
   What, have you lost your wits?
RODERIGO
   Most reverend signior, do you know my voice?
BRABANTIO
   Not I what are you?
RODERIGO
   My name is Roderigo.
BRABANTIO
   The worser welcome:
   I have charged thee not to haunt about my doors:
   In honest plainness thou hast heard me say

9

My daughter is not for thee; and now, in madness,
Being full of supper and distempering draughts,
Upon malicious bravery, dost thou come
To start my quiet.

RODERIGO

Sir, sir, sir,--

BRABANTIO

But thou must needs be sure
My spirit and my place have in them power
To make this bitter to thee.

RODERIGO

Patience, good sir.

BRABANTIO

What tell'st thou me of robbing? this is Venice;
My house is not a grange.

RODERIGO

Most grave Brabantio,
In simple and pure soul I come to you.

IAGO

'Zounds, sir, you are one of those that will not
serve God, if the devil bid you. Because we come to
do you service and you think we are ruffians, you'll
have your daughter covered with a Barbary horse;
you'll have your nephews neigh to you; you'll have
coursers for cousins and gennets for germans.

BRABANTIO

What profane wretch art thou?

IAGO

I am one, sir, that comes to tell you your daughter
and the Moor are now making the beast with two backs.

BRABANTIO

Thou art a villain.

IAGO

You are--a senator.

BRABANTIO
    This thou shalt answer; I know thee, Roderigo.
RODERIGO
    Sir, I will answer any thing. But, I beseech you,
    If't be your pleasure and most wise consent,
    As partly I find it is, that your fair daughter,
    At this odd-even and dull watch o' the night,
    Transported, with no worse nor better guard
    But with a knave of common hire, a gondolier,
    To the gross clasps of a lascivious Moor--
    If this be known to you and your allowance,
    We then have done you bold and saucy wrongs;
    But if you know not this, my manners tell me
    We have your wrong rebuke. Do not believe
    That, from the sense of all civility,
    I thus would play and trifle with your reverence:
    Your daughter, if you have not given her leave,
    I say again, hath made a gross revolt;
    Tying her duty, beauty, wit and fortunes
    In an extravagant and wheeling stranger
    Of here and every where. Straight satisfy yourself:
    If she be in her chamber or your house,
    Let loose on me the justice of the state
    For thus deluding you.
BRABANTIO
    Strike on the tinder, ho!
    Give me a taper! call up all my people!
    This accident is not unlike my dream:
    Belief of it oppresses me already.
    Light, I say! light!

                                    Exit above

IAGO
    Farewell; for I must leave you:

It seems not meet, nor wholesome to my place,
To be produced--as, if I stay, I shall--
Against the Moor: for, I do know, the state,
However this may gall him with some cheque,
Cannot with safety cast him, for he's embark'd
With such loud reason to the Cyprus wars,
Which even now stand in act, that, for their souls,
Another of his fathom they have none,
To lead their business: in which regard,
Though I do hate him as I do hell-pains.
Yet, for necessity of present life,
I must show out a flag and sign of love,
Which is indeed but sign. That you shall surely find him,
Lead to the Sagittary the raised search;
And there will I be with him. So, farewell.

Exit

Enter, below, BRABANTIO, and Servants with torches

BRABANTIO
It is too true an evil: gone she is;
And what's to come of my despised time
Is nought but bitterness. Now, Roderigo,
Where didst thou see her? O unhappy girl!
With the Moor, say'st thou? Who would be a father!
How didst thou know 'twas she? O she deceives me
Past thought! What said she to you? Get more tapers:
Raise all my kindred. Are they married, think you?
RODERIGO
Truly, I think they are.
BRABANTIO
O heaven! How got she out? O treason of the blood!

Fathers, from hence trust not your daughters' minds
By what you see them act. Is there not charms
By which the property of youth and maidhood
May be abused? Have you not read, Roderigo,
Of some such thing?

RODERIGO

Yes, sir, I have indeed.

BRABANTIO

Call up my brother. O, would you had had her!
Some one way, some another. Do you know
Where we may apprehend her and the Moor?

RODERIGO

I think I can discover him, if you please,
To get good guard and go along with me.

BRABANTIO

Pray you, lead on. At every house I'll call;
I may command at most. Get weapons, ho!
And raise some special officers of night.
On, good Roderigo: I'll deserve your pains.

Exeunt

SCENE II.

Another street.

Enter OTHELLO, IAGO, and Attendants with torches

IAGO

Though in the trade of war I have slain men,
Yet do I hold it very stuff o' the conscience
To do no contrived murder: I lack iniquity
Sometimes to do me service: nine or ten times
I had thought to have yerk'd him here under the ribs.

OTHELLO

'Tis better as it is.

IAGO

    Nay, but he prated,
    And spoke such scurvy and provoking terms
    Against your honour
    That, with the little godliness I have,
    I did full hard forbear him. But, I pray you, sir,
    Are you fast married? Be assured of this,
    That the magnifico is much beloved,
    And hath in his effect a voice potential
    As double as the duke's: he will divorce you;
    Or put upon you what restraint and grievance
    The law, with all his might to enforce it on,
    Will give him cable.

OTHELLO

    Let him do his spite:
    My services which I have done the signiory
    Shall out-tongue his complaints. 'Tis yet to know,--
    Which, when I know that boasting is an honour,
    I shall promulgate--I fetch my life and being
    From men of royal siege, and my demerits
    May speak unbonneted to as proud a fortune
    As this that I have reach'd: for know, Iago,
    But that I love the gentle Desdemona,
    I would not my unhoused free condition
    Put into circumscription and confine
    For the sea's worth. But, look! what lights come yond?

IAGO

    Those are the raised father and his friends:
    You were best go in.

OTHELLO

    Not I I must be found:
    My parts, my title and my perfect soul
    Shall manifest me rightly. Is it they?

IAGO

By Janus, I think no.

Enter CASSIO, and certain Officers with torches

OTHELLO
The servants of the duke, and my lieutenant.
The goodness of the night upon you, friends!
What is the news?
CASSIO
The duke does greet you, general,
And he requires your haste-post-haste appearance,
Even on the instant.
OTHELLO
What is the matter, think you?
CASSIO
Something from Cyprus as I may divine:
It is a business of some heat: the galleys
Have sent a dozen sequent messengers
This very night at one another's heels,
And many of the consuls, raised and met,
Are at the duke's already: you have been
hotly call'd for;
When, being not at your lodging to be found,
The senate hath sent about three several guests
To search you out.
OTHELLO
'Tis well I am found by you.
I will but spend a word here in the house,
And go with you.

Exit

CASSIO
Ancient, what makes he here?
IAGO

'Faith, he to-night hath boarded a land carack:
If it prove lawful prize, he's made for ever.
CASSIO
I do not understand.
IAGO
He's married.
CASSIO
To who?

Re-enter OTHELLO

IAGO
Marry, to--Come, captain, will you go?
OTHELLO
Have with you.
CASSIO
Here comes another troop to seek for you.
IAGO
It is Brabantio. General, be advised;
He comes to bad intent.

*Enter BRABANTIO, RODERIGO, and Officers with torches
and weapons*

OTHELLO
Holla! stand there!
RODERIGO
Signior, it is the Moor.
BRABANTIO
Down with him, thief!

They draw on both sides

IAGO
You, Roderigo! come, sir, I am for you.
OTHELLO

Keep up your bright swords, for the dew will rust them.
Good signior, you shall more command with years
Than with your weapons.

BRABANTIO

O thou foul thief, where hast thou stow'd my daughter?
Damn'd as thou art, thou hast enchanted her;
For I'll refer me to all things of sense,
If she in chains of magic were not bound,
Whether a maid so tender, fair and happy,
So opposite to marriage that she shunned
The wealthy curled darlings of our nation,
Would ever have, to incur a general mock,
Run from her guardage to the sooty bosom
Of such a thing as thou, to fear, not to delight.
Judge me the world, if 'tis not gross in sense
That thou hast practised on her with foul charms,
Abused her delicate youth with drugs or minerals
That weaken motion: I'll have't disputed on;
'Tis probable and palpable to thinking.
I therefore apprehend and do attach thee
For an abuser of the world, a practiser
Of arts inhibited and out of warrant.
Lay hold upon him: if he do resist,
Subdue him at his peril.

OTHELLO

Hold your hands,
Both you of my inclining, and the rest:
Were it my cue to fight, I should have known it
Without a prompter. Where will you that I go
To answer this your charge?

BRABANTIO

To prison, till fit time
Of law and course of direct session
Call thee to answer.

OTHELLO
  What if I do obey?
  How may the duke be therewith satisfied,
  Whose messengers are here about my side,
  Upon some present business of the state
  To bring me to him?
First Officer
  'Tis true, most worthy signior;
  The duke's in council and your noble self,
  I am sure, is sent for.
BRABANTIO
  How! the duke in council!
  In this time of the night! Bring him away:
  Mine's not an idle cause: the duke himself,
  Or any of my brothers of the state,
  Cannot but feel this wrong as 'twere their own;
  For if such actions may have passage free,
  Bond-slaves and pagans shall our statesmen be.

Exeunt

SCENE III.

A council-chamber.

The DUKE and Senators sitting at a table; Officers attending

DUKE OF VENICE
  There is no composition in these news
  That gives them credit.
First Senator
  Indeed, they are disproportion'd;
  My letters say a hundred and seven galleys.
DUKE OF VENICE
  And mine, a hundred and forty.

Second Senator

    And mine, two hundred:

    But though they jump not on a just account,--

    As in these cases, where the aim reports,

    'Tis oft with difference--yet do they all confirm

    A Turkish fleet, and bearing up to Cyprus.

DUKE OF VENICE

    Nay, it is possible enough to judgment:

    I do not so secure me in the error,

    But the main article I do approve

    In fearful sense.

Sailor

    [Within] What, ho! what, ho! what, ho!

First Officer

    A messenger from the galleys.

Enter a Sailor

DUKE OF VENICE

    Now, what's the business?

Sailor

    The Turkish preparation makes for Rhodes;

    So was I bid report here to the state

    By Signior Angelo.

DUKE OF VENICE

    How say you by this change?

First Senator

    This cannot be,

    By no assay of reason: 'tis a pageant,

    To keep us in false gaze. When we consider

    The importancy of Cyprus to the Turk,

    And let ourselves again but understand,

    That as it more concerns the Turk than Rhodes,

    So may he with more facile question bear it,

    For that it stands not in such warlike brace,

But altogether lacks the abilities
That Rhodes is dress'd in: if we make thought of this,
We must not think the Turk is so unskilful
To leave that latest which concerns him first,
Neglecting an attempt of ease and gain,
To wake and wage a danger profitless.

DUKE OF VENICE

Nay, in all confidence, he's not for Rhodes.

First Officer

Here is more news.

Enter a Messenger

Messenger

The Ottomites, reverend and gracious,
Steering with due course towards the isle of Rhodes,
Have there injointed them with an after fleet.

First Senator

Ay, so I thought. How many, as you guess?

Messenger

Of thirty sail: and now they do restem
Their backward course, bearing with frank appearance
Their purposes toward Cyprus. Signior Montano,
Your trusty and most valiant servitor,
With his free duty recommends you thus,
And prays you to believe him.

DUKE OF VENICE

'Tis certain, then, for Cyprus.
Marcus Luccicos, is not he in town?

First Senator

He's now in Florence.

DUKE OF VENICE

Write from us to him; post-post-haste dispatch.

First Senator

Here comes Brabantio and the valiant Moor.

*Enter BRABANTIO, OTHELLO, IAGO, RODERIGO, and
Officers*

DUKE OF VENICE
Valiant Othello, we must straight employ you
Against the general enemy Ottoman.

To BRABANTIO

I did not see you; welcome, gentle signior;
We lack'd your counsel and your help tonight.
BRABANTIO
So did I yours. Good your grace, pardon me;
Neither my place nor aught I heard of business
Hath raised me from my bed, nor doth the general care
Take hold on me, for my particular grief
Is of so flood-gate and o'erbearing nature
That it engluts and swallows other sorrows
And it is still itself.
DUKE OF VENICE
Why, what's the matter?
BRABANTIO
My daughter! O, my daughter!
DUKE OF VENICE Senator
Dead?
BRABANTIO
Ay, to me;
She is abused, stol'n from me, and corrupted
By spells and medicines bought of mountebanks;
For nature so preposterously to err,
Being not deficient, blind, or lame of sense,
Sans witchcraft could not.
DUKE OF VENICE
Whoe'er he be that in this foul proceeding
Hath thus beguiled your daughter of herself

And you of her, the bloody book of law
You shall yourself read in the bitter letter
After your own sense, yea, though our proper son
Stood in your action.

BRABANTIO

Humbly I thank your grace.
Here is the man, this Moor, whom now, it seems,
Your special mandate for the state-affairs
Hath hither brought.

DUKE OF VENICE Senator

We are very sorry for't.

DUKE OF VENICE

[To OTHELLO] What, in your own part, can you say to
this?

BRABANTIO

Nothing, but this is so.

OTHELLO

Most potent, grave, and reverend signiors,
My very noble and approved good masters,
That I have ta'en away this old man's daughter,
It is most true; true, I have married her:
The very head and front of my offending
Hath this extent, no more. Rude am I in my speech,
And little bless'd with the soft phrase of peace:
For since these arms of mine had seven years' pith,
Till now some nine moons wasted, they have used
Their dearest action in the tented field,
And little of this great world can I speak,
More than pertains to feats of broil and battle,
And therefore little shall I grace my cause
In speaking for myself. Yet, by your gracious patience,
I will a round unvarnish'd tale deliver
Of my whole course of love; what drugs, what charms,
What conjuration and what mighty magic,

For such proceeding I am charged withal,
I won his daughter.

BRABANTIO

A maiden never bold;
Of spirit so still and quiet, that her motion
Blush'd at herself; and she, in spite of nature,
Of years, of country, credit, every thing,
To fall in love with what she fear'd to look on!
It is a judgment maim'd and most imperfect
That will confess perfection so could err
Against all rules of nature, and must be driven
To find out practises of cunning hell,
Why this should be. I therefore vouch again
That with some mixtures powerful o'er the blood,
Or with some dram conjured to this effect,
He wrought upon her.

DUKE OF VENICE

To vouch this, is no proof,
Without more wider and more overt test
Than these thin habits and poor likelihoods
Of modern seeming do prefer against him.

First Senator

But, Othello, speak:
Did you by indirect and forced courses
Subdue and poison this young maid's affections?
Or came it by request and such fair question
As soul to soul affordeth?

OTHELLO

I do beseech you,
Send for the lady to the Sagittary,
And let her speak of me before her father:
If you do find me foul in her report,
The trust, the office I do hold of you,
Not only take away, but let your sentence

Even fall upon my life.
DUKE OF VENICE
Fetch Desdemona hither.
OTHELLO
Ancient, conduct them: you best know the place.

Exeunt IAGO and Attendants

And, till she come, as truly as to heaven
I do confess the vices of my blood,
So justly to your grave ears I'll present
How I did thrive in this fair lady's love,
And she in mine.
DUKE OF VENICE
Say it, Othello.
OTHELLO
Her father loved me; oft invited me;
Still question'd me the story of my life,
From year to year, the battles, sieges, fortunes,
That I have passed.
I ran it through, even from my boyish days,
To the very moment that he bade me tell it;
Wherein I spake of most disastrous chances,
Of moving accidents by flood and field
Of hair-breadth scapes i' the imminent deadly breach,
Of being taken by the insolent foe
And sold to slavery, of my redemption thence
And portance in my travels' history:
Wherein of antres vast and deserts idle,
Rough quarries, rocks and hills whose heads touch
heaven
It was my hint to speak,--such was the process;
And of the Cannibals that each other eat,
The Anthropophagi and men whose heads
Do grow beneath their shoulders. This to hear

Would Desdemona seriously incline:
But still the house-affairs would draw her thence:
Which ever as she could with haste dispatch,
She'ld come again, and with a greedy ear
Devour up my discourse: which I observing,
Took once a pliant hour, and found good means
To draw from her a prayer of earnest heart
That I would all my pilgrimage dilate,
Whereof by parcels she had something heard,
But not intentively: I did consent,
And often did beguile her of her tears,
When I did speak of some distressful stroke
That my youth suffer'd. My story being done,
She gave me for my pains a world of sighs:
She swore, in faith, twas strange, 'twas passing strange,
'Twas pitiful, 'twas wondrous pitiful:
She wish'd she had not heard it, yet she wish'd
That heaven had made her such a man: she thank'd me,
And bade me, if I had a friend that loved her,
I should but teach him how to tell my story.
And that would woo her. Upon this hint I spake:
She loved me for the dangers I had pass'd,
And I loved her that she did pity them.
This only is the witchcraft I have used:
Here comes the lady; let her witness it.

Enter DESDEMONA, IAGO, and Attendants

DUKE OF VENICE
    I think this tale would win my daughter too.
    Good Brabantio,
    Take up this mangled matter at the best:
    Men do their broken weapons rather use
    Than their bare hands.
BRABANTIO

I pray you, hear her speak:
If she confess that she was half the wooer,
Destruction on my head, if my bad blame
Light on the man! Come hither, gentle mistress:
Do you perceive in all this noble company
Where most you owe obedience?

DESDEMONA

My noble father,
I do perceive here a divided duty:
To you I am bound for life and education;
My life and education both do learn me
How to respect you; you are the lord of duty;
I am hitherto your daughter: but here's my husband,
And so much duty as my mother show'd
To you, preferring you before her father,
So much I challenge that I may profess
Due to the Moor my lord.

BRABANTIO

God be wi' you! I have done.
Please it your grace, on to the state-affairs:
I had rather to adopt a child than get it.
Come hither, Moor:
I here do give thee that with all my heart
Which, but thou hast already, with all my heart
I would keep from thee. For your sake, jewel,
I am glad at soul I have no other child:
For thy escape would teach me tyranny,
To hang clogs on them. I have done, my lord.

DUKE OF VENICE

Let me speak like yourself, and lay a sentence,
Which, as a grise or step, may help these lovers
Into your favour.
When remedies are past, the griefs are ended
By seeing the worst, which late on hopes depended.

To mourn a mischief that is past and gone
Is the next way to draw new mischief on.
What cannot be preserved when fortune takes
Patience her injury a mockery makes.
The robb'd that smiles steals something from the thief;
He robs himself that spends a bootless grief.

BRABANTIO

So let the Turk of Cyprus us beguile;
We lose it not, so long as we can smile.
He bears the sentence well that nothing bears
But the free comfort which from thence he hears,
But he bears both the sentence and the sorrow
That, to pay grief, must of poor patience borrow.
These sentences, to sugar, or to gall,
Being strong on both sides, are equivocal:
But words are words; I never yet did hear
That the bruised heart was pierced through the ear.
I humbly beseech you, proceed to the affairs of state.

DUKE OF VENICE

The Turk with a most mighty preparation makes for
Cyprus. Othello, the fortitude of the place is best
known to you; and though we have there a substitute
of most allowed sufficiency, yet opinion, a
sovereign mistress of effects, throws a more safer
voice on you: you must therefore be content to
slubber the gloss of your new fortunes with this
more stubborn and boisterous expedition.

OTHELLO

The tyrant custom, most grave senators,
Hath made the flinty and steel couch of war
My thrice-driven bed of down: I do agnise
A natural and prompt alacrity
I find in hardness, and do undertake
These present wars against the Ottomites.

Most humbly therefore bending to your state,
I crave fit disposition for my wife.
Due reference of place and exhibition,
With such accommodation and besort
As levels with her breeding.

DUKE OF VENICE

If you please,
Be't at her father's.

BRABANTIO

I'll not have it so.

OTHELLO

Nor I.

DESDEMONA

Nor I; I would not there reside,
To put my father in impatient thoughts
By being in his eye. Most gracious duke,
To my unfolding lend your prosperous ear;
And let me find a charter in your voice,
To assist my simpleness.

DUKE OF VENICE

What would You, Desdemona?

DESDEMONA

That I did love the Moor to live with him,
My downright violence and storm of fortunes
May trumpet to the world: my heart's subdued
Even to the very quality of my lord:
I saw Othello's visage in his mind,
And to his honour and his valiant parts
Did I my soul and fortunes consecrate.
So that, dear lords, if I be left behind,
A moth of peace, and he go to the war,
The rites for which I love him are bereft me,
And I a heavy interim shall support
By his dear absence. Let me go with him.

OTHELLO

    Let her have your voices.

    Vouch with me, heaven, I therefore beg it not,

    To please the palate of my appetite,

    Nor to comply with heat--the young affects

    In me defunct--and proper satisfaction.

    But to be free and bounteous to her mind:

    And heaven defend your good souls, that you think

    I will your serious and great business scant

    For she is with me: no, when light-wing'd toys

    Of feather'd Cupid seal with wanton dullness

    My speculative and officed instruments,

    That my disports corrupt and taint my business,

    Let housewives make a skillet of my helm,

    And all indign and base adversities

    Make head against my estimation!

DUKE OF VENICE

    Be it as you shall privately determine,

    Either for her stay or going: the affair cries haste,

    And speed must answer it.

First Senator

    You must away to-night.

OTHELLO

    With all my heart.

DUKE OF VENICE

    At nine i' the morning here we'll meet again.

    Othello, leave some officer behind,

    And he shall our commission bring to you;

    With such things else of quality and respect

    As doth import you.

OTHELLO

    So please your grace, my ancient;

    A man he is of honest and trust:

    To his conveyance I assign my wife,

29

With what else needful your good grace shall think
To be sent after me.
DUKE OF VENICE
Let it be so.
Good night to every one.

To BRABANTIO

And, noble signior,
If virtue no delighted beauty lack,
Your son-in-law is far more fair than black.
First Senator
Adieu, brave Moor, use Desdemona well.
BRABANTIO
Look to her, Moor, if thou hast eyes to see:
She has deceived her father, and may thee.

Exeunt DUKE OF VENICE, Senators, Officers, & c

OTHELLO
My life upon her faith! Honest Iago,
My Desdemona must I leave to thee:
I prithee, let thy wife attend on her:
And bring them after in the best advantage.
Come, Desdemona: I have but an hour
Of love, of worldly matters and direction,
To spend with thee: we must obey the time.

Exeunt OTHELLO and DESDEMONA

RODERIGO
Iago,--
IAGO
What say'st thou, noble heart?
RODERIGO
What will I do, thinkest thou?

IAGO

Why, go to bed, and sleep.

RODERIGO

I will incontinently drown myself.

IAGO

If thou dost, I shall never love thee after. Why,
thou silly gentleman!

RODERIGO

It is silliness to live when to live is torment; and
then have we a prescription to die when death is our
physician.

IAGO

O villainous! I have looked upon the world for four
times seven years; and since I could distinguish
betwixt a benefit and an injury, I never found man
that knew how to love himself. Ere I would say, I
would drown myself for the love of a guinea-hen, I
would change my humanity with a baboon.

RODERIGO

What should I do? I confess it is my shame to be so
fond; but it is not in my virtue to amend it.

IAGO

Virtue! a fig! 'tis in ourselves that we are thus
or thus. Our bodies are our gardens, to the which
our wills are gardeners: so that if we will plant
nettles, or sow lettuce, set hyssop and weed up
thyme, supply it with one gender of herbs, or
distract it with many, either to have it sterile
with idleness, or manured with industry, why, the
power and corrigible authority of this lies in our
wills. If the balance of our lives had not one
scale of reason to poise another of sensuality, the
blood and baseness of our natures would conduct us
to most preposterous conclusions: but we have

reason to cool our raging motions, our carnal
stings, our unbitted lusts, whereof I take this that
you call love to be a sect or scion.

RODERIGO

It cannot be.

IAGO

It is merely a lust of the blood and a permission of
the will. Come, be a man. Drown thyself! drown
cats and blind puppies. I have professed me thy
friend and I confess me knit to thy deserving with
cables of perdurable toughness; I could never
better stead thee than now. Put money in thy
purse; follow thou the wars; defeat thy favour with
an usurped beard; I say, put money in thy purse. It
cannot be that Desdemona should long continue her
love to the Moor,-- put money in thy purse,--nor he
his to her: it was a violent commencement, and thou
shalt see an answerable sequestration:--put but
money in thy purse. These Moors are changeable in
their wills: fill thy purse with money:--the food
that to him now is as luscious as locusts, shall be
to him shortly as bitter as coloquintida. She must
change for youth: when she is sated with his body,
she will find the error of her choice: she must
have change, she must: therefore put money in thy
purse. If thou wilt needs damn thyself, do it a
more delicate way than drowning. Make all the money
thou canst: if sanctimony and a frail vow betwixt
an erring barbarian and a supersubtle Venetian not
too hard for my wits and all the tribe of hell, thou
shalt enjoy her; therefore make money. A pox of
drowning thyself! it is clean out of the way: seek
thou rather to be hanged in compassing thy joy than
to be drowned and go without her.

RODERIGO

Wilt thou be fast to my hopes, if I depend on
the issue?

IAGO

Thou art sure of me:--go, make money:--I have told
thee often, and I re-tell thee again and again, I
hate the Moor: my cause is hearted; thine hath no
less reason. Let us be conjunctive in our revenge
against him: if thou canst cuckold him, thou dost
thyself a pleasure, me a sport. There are many
events in the womb of time which will be delivered.
Traverse! go, provide thy money. We will have more
of this to-morrow. Adieu.

RODERIGO

Where shall we meet i' the morning?

IAGO

At my lodging.

RODERIGO

I'll be with thee betimes.

IAGO

Go to; farewell. Do you hear, Roderigo?

RODERIGO

What say you?

IAGO

No more of drowning, do you hear?

RODERIGO

I am changed: I'll go sell all my land.

Exit

IAGO

Thus do I ever make my fool my purse:
For I mine own gain'd knowledge should profane,
If I would time expend with such a snipe.
But for my sport and profit. I hate the Moor:

33

And it is thought abroad, that 'twixt my sheets
He has done my office: I know not if't be true;
But I, for mere suspicion in that kind,
Will do as if for surety. He holds me well;
The better shall my purpose work on him.
Cassio's a proper man: let me see now:
To get his place and to plume up my will
In double knavery--How, how? Let's see:--
After some time, to abuse Othello's ear
That he is too familiar with his wife.
He hath a person and a smooth dispose
To be suspected, framed to make women false.
The Moor is of a free and open nature,
That thinks men honest that but seem to be so,
And will as tenderly be led by the nose
As asses are.
I have't. It is engender'd. Hell and night
Must bring this monstrous birth to the world's light.

Exit

ACT II

SCENE I.

A Sea-port in Cyprus. An open place near the quay.

Enter MONTANO and two Gentlemen

MONTANO
  What from the cape can you discern at sea?
First Gentleman
  Nothing at all: it is a highwrought flood;
  I cannot, 'twixt the heaven and the main,
  Descry a sail.
MONTANO
  Methinks the wind hath spoke aloud at land;
  A fuller blast ne'er shook our battlements:
  If it hath ruffian'd so upon the sea,
  What ribs of oak, when mountains melt on them,
  Can hold the mortise? What shall we hear of this?
Second Gentleman
  A segregation of the Turkish fleet:
  For do but stand upon the foaming shore,
  The chidden billow seems to pelt the clouds;
  The wind-shaked surge, with high and monstrous mane,
  seems to cast water on the burning bear,
  And quench the guards of the ever-fixed pole:
  I never did like molestation view
  On the enchafed flood.
MONTANO
  If that the Turkish fleet
  Be not enshelter'd and embay'd, they are drown'd:
  It is impossible they bear it out.
  Enter a third Gentleman

35

Third Gentleman
> News, lads! our wars are done.
> The desperate tempest hath so bang'd the Turks,
> That their designment halts: a noble ship of Venice
> Hath seen a grievous wreck and sufferance
> On most part of their fleet.

MONTANO
> How! is this true?

Third Gentleman
> The ship is here put in,
> A Veronesa; Michael Cassio,
> Lieutenant to the warlike Moor Othello,
> Is come on shore: the Moor himself at sea,
> And is in full commission here for Cyprus.

MONTANO
> I am glad on't; 'tis a worthy governor.

Third Gentleman
> But this same Cassio, though he speak of comfort
> Touching the Turkish loss, yet he looks sadly,
> And prays the Moor be safe; for they were parted
> With foul and violent tempest.

MONTANO
> Pray heavens he be;
> For I have served him, and the man commands
> Like a full soldier. Let's to the seaside, ho!
> As well to see the vessel that's come in
> As to throw out our eyes for brave Othello,
> Even till we make the main and the aerial blue
> An indistinct regard.

Third Gentleman
> Come, let's do so:
> For every minute is expectancy
> Of more arrivance.

Enter CASSIO

CASSIO

Thanks, you the valiant of this warlike isle,
That so approve the Moor! O, let the heavens
Give him defence against the elements,
For I have lost us him on a dangerous sea.

MONTANO

Is he well shipp'd?

CASSIO

His bark is stoutly timber'd, his pilot
Of very expert and approved allowance;
Therefore my hopes, not surfeited to death,
Stand in bold cure.

A cry within 'A sail, a sail, a sail!'

Enter a fourth Gentleman

CASSIO

What noise?

Fourth Gentleman

The town is empty; on the brow o' the sea
Stand ranks of people, and they cry 'A sail!'

CASSIO

My hopes do shape him for the governor.
Guns heard

Second Gentlemen

They do discharge their shot of courtesy:
Our friends at least.

CASSIO

I pray you, sir, go forth,
And give us truth who 'tis that is arrived.

Second Gentleman

I shall.

Exit

MONTANO
  But, good lieutenant, is your general wived?
CASSIO
  Most fortunately: he hath achieved a maid
  That paragons description and wild fame;
  One that excels the quirks of blazoning pens,
  And in the essential vesture of creation
  Does tire the ingener.

Re-enter Second Gentleman

  How now! who has put in?
Second Gentleman
  'Tis one Iago, ancient to the general.
CASSIO
  Has had most favourable and happy speed:
  Tempests themselves, high seas, and howling winds,
  The gutter'd rocks and congregated sands--
  Traitors ensteep'd to clog the guiltless keel,--
  As having sense of beauty, do omit
  Their mortal natures, letting go safely by
  The divine Desdemona.
MONTANO
  What is she?
CASSIO
  She that I spake of, our great captain's captain,
  Left in the conduct of the bold Iago,
  Whose footing here anticipates our thoughts
  A se'nnight's speed. Great Jove, Othello guard,
  And swell his sail with thine own powerful breath,
  That he may bless this bay with his tall ship,

Make love's quick pants in Desdemona's arms,
Give renew'd fire to our extincted spirits
And bring all Cyprus comfort!

Enter DESDEMONA, EMILIA, IAGO, RODERIGO, and Attendants

O, behold,
The riches of the ship is come on shore!
Ye men of Cyprus, let her have your knees.
Hail to thee, lady! and the grace of heaven,
Before, behind thee, and on every hand,
Enwheel thee round!
DESDEMONA
I thank you, valiant Cassio.
What tidings can you tell me of my lord?
CASSIO
He is not yet arrived: nor know I aught
But that he's well and will be shortly here.
DESDEMONA
O, but I fear--How lost you company?
CASSIO
The great contention of the sea and skies
Parted our fellowship--But, hark! a sail.

Within 'A sail, a sail!' Guns heard

Second Gentleman
They give their greeting to the citadel;
This likewise is a friend.
CASSIO
See for the news.

Exit Gentleman

Good ancient, you are welcome.

To EMILIA

Welcome, mistress.
Let it not gall your patience, good Iago,
That I extend my manners; 'tis my breeding
That gives me this bold show of courtesy.

Kissing her

IAGO

Sir, would she give you so much of her lips
As of her tongue she oft bestows on me,
You'll have enough.

DESDEMONA

Alas, she has no speech.

IAGO

In faith, too much;
I find it still, when I have list to sleep:
Marry, before your ladyship, I grant,
She puts her tongue a little in her heart,
And chides with thinking.

EMILIA

You have little cause to say so.

IAGO

Come on, come on; you are pictures out of doors,
Bells in your parlors, wild-cats in your kitchens,
Saints m your injuries, devils being offended,
Players in your housewifery, and housewives' in your
beds.

DESDEMONA

O, fie upon thee, slanderer!

IAGO

Nay, it is true, or else I am a Turk:
You rise to play and go to bed to work.

EMILIA

You shall not write my praise.

IAGO

No, let me not.

DESDEMONA

What wouldst thou write of me, if thou shouldst
praise me?

IAGO

O gentle lady, do not put me to't;

For I am nothing, if not critical.

DESDEMONA

Come on assay. There's one gone to the harbour?

IAGO

Ay, madam.

DESDEMONA

I am not merry; but I do beguile

The thing I am, by seeming otherwise.

Come, how wouldst thou praise me?

IAGO

I am about it; but indeed my invention

Comes from my pate as birdlime does from frize;

It plucks out brains and all: but my Muse labours,

And thus she is deliver'd.

If she be fair and wise, fairness and wit,

The one's for use, the other useth it.

DESDEMONA

Well praised! How if she be black and witty?

IAGO

If she be black, and thereto have a wit,

She'll find a white that shall her blackness fit.

DESDEMONA

Worse and worse.

EMILIA

How if fair and foolish?

IAGO

She never yet was foolish that was fair;
For even her folly help'd her to an heir.

DESDEMONA

These are old fond paradoxes to make fools laugh i'
the alehouse. What miserable praise hast thou for
her that's foul and foolish?

IAGO

There's none so foul and foolish thereunto,
But does foul pranks which fair and wise ones do.

DESDEMONA

O heavy ignorance! thou praisest the worst best.
But what praise couldst thou bestow on a deserving
woman indeed, one that, in the authority of her
merit, did justly put on the vouch of very malice itself?

IAGO

She that was ever fair and never proud,
Had tongue at will and yet was never loud,
Never lack'd gold and yet went never gay,
Fled from her wish and yet said 'Now I may,'
She that being anger'd, her revenge being nigh,
Bade her wrong stay and her displeasure fly,
She that in wisdom never was so frail
To change the cod's head for the salmon's tail;
She that could think and ne'er disclose her mind,
See suitors following and not look behind,
She was a wight, if ever such wight were,--

DESDEMONA

To do what?

IAGO

To suckle fools and chronicle small beer.

DESDEMONA

O most lame and impotent conclusion! Do not learn
of him, Emilia, though he be thy husband. How say
you, Cassio? is he not a most profane and liberal

counsellor?

CASSIO

He speaks home, madam: You may relish him more in
the soldier than in the scholar.

IAGO

[Aside] He takes her by the palm: ay, well said,
whisper: with as little a web as this will I
ensnare as great a fly as Cassio. Ay, smile upon
her, do; I will gyve thee in thine own courtship.
You say true; 'tis so, indeed: if such tricks as
these strip you out of your lieutenantry, it had
been better you had not kissed your three fingers so
oft, which now again you are most apt to play the
sir in. Very good; well kissed! an excellent
courtesy! 'tis so, indeed. Yet again your fingers
to your lips? would they were clyster-pipes for your
sake!

Trumpet within

The Moor! I know his trumpet.

CASSIO

'Tis truly so.

DESDEMONA

Let's meet him and receive him.

CASSIO

Lo, where he comes!

Enter OTHELLO and Attendants

OTHELLO

O my fair warrior!

DESDEMONA

My dear Othello!

OTHELLO

It gives me wonder great as my content
To see you here before me. O my soul's joy!
If after every tempest come such calms,
May the winds blow till they have waken'd death!
And let the labouring bark climb hills of seas
Olympus-high and duck again as low
As hell's from heaven! If it were now to die,
'Twere now to be most happy; for, I fear,
My soul hath her content so absolute
That not another comfort like to this
Succeeds in unknown fate.

DESDEMONA

The heavens forbid
But that our loves and comforts should increase,
Even as our days do grow!

OTHELLO

Amen to that, sweet powers!
I cannot speak enough of this content;
It stops me here; it is too much of joy:
And this, and this, the greatest discords be

Kissing her

That e'er our hearts shall make!

IAGO

[Aside] O, you are well tuned now!
But I'll set down the pegs that make this music,
As honest as I am.

OTHELLO

Come, let us to the castle.
News, friends; our wars are done, the Turks
are drown'd.
How does my old acquaintance of this isle?
Honey, you shall be well desired in Cyprus;
I have found great love amongst them. O my sweet,

I prattle out of fashion, and I dote
In mine own comforts. I prithee, good Iago,
Go to the bay and disembark my coffers:
Bring thou the master to the citadel;
He is a good one, and his worthiness
Does challenge much respect. Come, Desdemona,
Once more, well met at Cyprus.

Exeunt OTHELLO, DESDEMONA, and Attendants

IAGO

Do thou meet me presently at the harbour. Come
hither. If thou be'st valiant,-- as, they say, base
men being in love have then a nobility in their
natures more than is native to them--list me. The
lieutenant tonight watches on the court of
guard:--first, I must tell thee this--Desdemona is
directly in love with him.

RODERIGO

With him! why, 'tis not possible.

IAGO

Lay thy finger thus, and let thy soul be instructed.
Mark me with what violence she first loved the Moor,
but for bragging and telling her fantastical lies:
and will she love him still for prating? let not
thy discreet heart think it. Her eye must be fed;
and what delight shall she have to look on the
devil? When the blood is made dull with the act of
sport, there should be, again to inflame it and to
give satiety a fresh appetite, loveliness in favour,
sympathy in years, manners and beauties; all which
the Moor is defective in: now, for want of these
required conveniences, her delicate tenderness will
find itself abused, begin to heave the gorge,
disrelish and abhor the Moor; very nature will

instruct her in it and compel her to some second
choice. Now, sir, this granted,--as it is a most
pregnant and unforced position--who stands so
eminent in the degree of this fortune as Cassio
does? a knave very voluble; no further
conscionable than in putting on the mere form of
civil and humane seeming, for the better compassing
of his salt and most hidden loose affection? why,
none; why, none: a slipper and subtle knave, a
finder of occasions, that has an eye can stamp and
counterfeit advantages, though true advantage never
present itself; a devilish knave. Besides, the
knave is handsome, young, and hath all those
requisites in him that folly and green minds look
after: a pestilent complete knave; and the woman
hath found him already.

RODERIGO

I cannot believe that in her; she's full of
most blessed condition.

IAGO

Blessed fig's-end! the wine she drinks is made of
grapes: if she had been blessed, she would never
have loved the Moor. Blessed pudding! Didst thou
not see her paddle with the palm of his hand? didst
not mark that?

RODERIGO

Yes, that I did; but that was but courtesy.

IAGO

Lechery, by this hand; an index and obscure prologue
to the history of lust and foul thoughts. They met
so near with their lips that their breaths embraced
together. Villanous thoughts, Roderigo! when these
mutualities so marshal the way, hard at hand comes
the master and main exercise, the incorporate

conclusion, Pish! But, sir, be you ruled by me: I
have brought you from Venice. Watch you to-night;
for the command, I'll lay't upon you. Cassio knows
you not. I'll not be far from you: do you find
some occasion to anger Cassio, either by speaking
too loud, or tainting his discipline; or from what
other course you please, which the time shall more
favourably minister.

RODERIGO

Well.

IAGO

Sir, he is rash and very sudden in choler, and haply
may strike at you: provoke him, that he may; for
even out of that will I cause these of Cyprus to
mutiny; whose qualification shall come into no true
taste again but by the displanting of Cassio. So
shall you have a shorter journey to your desires by
the means I shall then have to prefer them; and the
impediment most profitably removed, without the
which there were no expectation of our prosperity.

RODERIGO

I will do this, if I can bring it to any
opportunity.

IAGO

I warrant thee. Meet me by and by at the citadel:
I must fetch his necessaries ashore. Farewell.

RODERIGO

Adieu.

Exit

IAGO

That Cassio loves her, I do well believe it;
That she loves him, 'tis apt and of great credit:
The Moor, howbeit that I endure him not,

Is of a constant, loving, noble nature,
And I dare think he'll prove to Desdemona
A most dear husband. Now, I do love her too;
Not out of absolute lust, though peradventure
I stand accountant for as great a sin,
But partly led to diet my revenge,
For that I do suspect the lusty Moor
Hath leap'd into my seat; the thought whereof
Doth, like a poisonous mineral, gnaw my inwards;
And nothing can or shall content my soul
Till I am even'd with him, wife for wife,
Or failing so, yet that I put the Moor
At least into a jealousy so strong
That judgment cannot cure. Which thing to do,
If this poor trash of Venice, whom I trash
For his quick hunting, stand the putting on,
I'll have our Michael Cassio on the hip,
Abuse him to the Moor in the rank garb--
For I fear Cassio with my night-cap too--
Make the Moor thank me, love me and reward me.
For making him egregiously an ass
And practising upon his peace and quiet
Even to madness. 'Tis here, but yet confused:
Knavery's plain face is never seen tin used.

Exit

SCENE II.

A street.

Enter a Herald with a proclamation; People following

Herald
    It is Othello's pleasure, our noble and valiant
    general, that, upon certain tidings now arrived,

importing the mere perdition of the Turkish fleet,
every man put himself into triumph; some to dance,
some to make bonfires, each man to what sport and
revels his addiction leads him: for, besides these
beneficial news, it is the celebration of his
nuptial. So much was his pleasure should be
proclaimed. All offices are open, and there is full
liberty of feasting from this present hour of five
till the bell have told eleven. Heaven bless the
isle of Cyprus and our noble general Othello!

Exeunt

SCENE III.

A hall in the castle.

Enter OTHELLO, DESDEMONA, CASSIO, and Attendants

OTHELLO

Good Michael, look you to the guard to-night:
Let's teach ourselves that honourable stop,
Not to outsport discretion.

CASSIO

Iago hath direction what to do;
But, notwithstanding, with my personal eye
Will I look to't.

OTHELLO

Iago is most honest.
Michael, good night: to-morrow with your earliest
Let me have speech with you.

To DESDEMONA

Come, my dear love,
The purchase made, the fruits are to ensue;

That profit's yet to come 'tween me and you.
Good night.

Exeunt OTHELLO, DESDEMONA, and Attendants

Enter IAGO

CASSIO
Welcome, Iago; we must to the watch.
IAGO
Not this hour, lieutenant; 'tis not yet ten o' the
clock. Our general cast us thus early for the love
of his Desdemona; who let us not therefore blame:
he hath not yet made wanton the night with her; and
she is sport for Jove.
CASSIO
She's a most exquisite lady.
IAGO
And, I'll warrant her, fun of game.
CASSIO
Indeed, she's a most fresh and delicate creature.
IAGO
What an eye she has! methinks it sounds a parley of
provocation.
CASSIO
An inviting eye; and yet methinks right modest.
IAGO
And when she speaks, is it not an alarum to love?
CASSIO
She is indeed perfection.
IAGO
Well, happiness to their sheets! Come, lieutenant, I
have a stoup of wine; and here without are a brace
of Cyprus gallants that would fain have a measure to

the health of black Othello.

CASSIO

Not to-night, good Iago: I have very poor and
unhappy brains for drinking: I could well wish
courtesy would invent some other custom of
entertainment.

IAGO

O, they are our friends; but one cup: I'll drink for
you.

CASSIO

I have drunk but one cup to-night, and that was
craftily qualified too, and, behold, what innovation
it makes here: I am unfortunate in the infirmity,
and dare not task my weakness with any more.

IAGO

What, man! 'tis a night of revels: the gallants
desire it.

CASSIO

Where are they?

IAGO

Here at the door; I pray you, call them in.

CASSIO

I'll do't; but it dislikes me.

Exit

IAGO

If I can fasten but one cup upon him,
With that which he hath drunk to-night already,
He'll be as full of quarrel and offence
As my young mistress' dog. Now, my sick fool
Roderigo,
Whom love hath turn'd almost the wrong side out,
To Desdemona hath to-night caroused
Potations pottle-deep; and he's to watch:

Three lads of Cyprus, noble swelling spirits,
That hold their honours in a wary distance,
The very elements of this warlike isle,
Have I to-night fluster'd with flowing cups,
And they watch too. Now, 'mongst this flock of
drunkards,
Am I to put our Cassio in some action
That may offend the isle.--But here they come:
If consequence do but approve my dream,
My boat sails freely, both with wind and stream.

Re-enter CASSIO; with him MONTANO and Gentlemen;
servants following with wine

CASSIO
'Fore God, they have given me a rouse already.
MONTANO
Good faith, a little one; not past a pint, as I am
a soldier.
IAGO
Some wine, ho!

Sings

And let me the canakin clink, clink;
And let me the canakin clink
A soldier's a man;
A life's but a span;
Why, then, let a soldier drink.
Some wine, boys!
CASSIO
'Fore God, an excellent song.
IAGO
I learned it in England, where, indeed, they are
most potent in potting: your Dane, your German, and

your swag-bellied Hollander--Drink, ho!--are nothing
to your English.

CASSIO

Is your Englishman so expert in his drinking?

IAGO

Why, he drinks you, with facility, your Dane dead
drunk; he sweats not to overthrow your Almain; he
gives your Hollander a vomit, ere the next pottle
can be filled.

CASSIO

To the health of our general!

MONTANO

I am for it, lieutenant; and I'll do you justice.

IAGO

O sweet England!
King Stephen was a worthy peer,
His breeches cost him but a crown;
He held them sixpence all too dear,
With that he call'd the tailor lown.
He was a wight of high renown,
And thou art but of low degree:
'Tis pride that pulls the country down;
Then take thine auld cloak about thee.
Some wine, ho!

CASSIO

Why, this is a more exquisite song than the other.

IAGO

Will you hear't again?

CASSIO

No; for I hold him to be unworthy of his place that
does those things. Well, God's above all; and there
be souls must be saved, and there be souls must not be
saved.

IAGO

It's true, good lieutenant.

CASSIO

For mine own part,--no offence to the general, nor
any man of quality,--I hope to be saved.

IAGO

And so do I too, lieutenant.

CASSIO

Ay, but, by your leave, not before me; the
lieutenant is to be saved before the ancient. Let's
have no more of this; let's to our affairs.--Forgive
us our sins!--Gentlemen, let's look to our business.
Do not think, gentlemen. I am drunk: this is my
ancient; this is my right hand, and this is my left:
I am not drunk now; I can stand well enough, and
speak well enough.

All

Excellent well.

CASSIO

Why, very well then; you must not think then that I am
drunk.

Exit

MONTANO

To the platform, masters; come, let's set the watch.

IAGO

You see this fellow that is gone before;
He is a soldier fit to stand by Caesar
And give direction: and do but see his vice;
'Tis to his virtue a just equinox,
The one as long as the other: 'tis pity of him.
I fear the trust Othello puts him in.
On some odd time of his infirmity,
Will shake this island.

MONTANO

But is he often thus?

IAGO

'Tis evermore the prologue to his sleep:
He'll watch the horologe a double set,
If drink rock not his cradle.

MONTANO

It were well
The general were put in mind of it.
Perhaps he sees it not; or his good nature
Prizes the virtue that appears in Cassio,
And looks not on his evils: is not this true?

Enter RODERIGO

IAGO

[Aside to him] How now, Roderigo!
I pray you, after the lieutenant; go.

Exit RODERIGO

MONTANO

And 'tis great pity that the noble Moor
Should hazard such a place as his own second
With one of an ingraft infirmity:
It were an honest action to say
So to the Moor.

IAGO

Not I, for this fair island:
I do love Cassio well; and would do much
To cure him of this evil--But, hark! what noise?

Cry within: 'Help! help!'

Re-enter CASSIO, driving in RODERIGO

CASSIO

55

You rogue! you rascal!

MONTANO

What's the matter, lieutenant?

CASSIO

A knave teach me my duty!

I'll beat the knave into a twiggen bottle.

RODERIGO

Beat me!

CASSIO

Dost thou prate, rogue?

Striking RODERIGO

MONTANO

Nay, good lieutenant;

Staying him

I pray you, sir, hold your hand.

CASSIO

Let me go, sir,

Or I'll knock you o'er the mazzard.

MONTANO

Come, come,

you're drunk.

CASSIO

Drunk!

They fight

IAGO

[Aside to RODERIGO] Away, I say; go out, and cry a mutiny.

Exit RODERIGO

Nay, good lieutenant,--alas, gentlemen;--

Help, ho!--Lieutenant,--sir,--Montano,--sir;
Help, masters!--Here's a goodly watch indeed!

Bell rings

Who's that which rings the bell?--Diablo, ho!
The town will rise: God's will, lieutenant, hold!
You will be shamed for ever.

Re-enter OTHELLO and Attendants

OTHELLO
What is the matter here?
MONTANO
'Zounds, I bleed still; I am hurt to the death.

Faints

OTHELLO
Hold, for your lives!
IAGO
Hold, ho! Lieutenant,--sir--Montano,--gentlemen,--
Have you forgot all sense of place and duty?
Hold! the general speaks to you; hold, hold, for shame!
OTHELLO
Why, how now, ho! from whence ariseth this?
Are we turn'd Turks, and to ourselves do that
Which heaven hath forbid the Ottomites?
For Christian shame, put by this barbarous brawl:
He that stirs next to carve for his own rage
Holds his soul light; he dies upon his motion.
Silence that dreadful bell: it frights the isle
From her propriety. What is the matter, masters?
Honest Iago, that look'st dead with grieving,
Speak, who began this? on thy love, I charge thee.
IAGO

I do not know: friends all but now, even now,
In quarter, and in terms like bride and groom
Devesting them for bed; and then, but now--
As if some planet had unwitted men--
Swords out, and tilting one at other's breast,
In opposition bloody. I cannot speak
Any beginning to this peevish odds;
And would in action glorious I had lost
Those legs that brought me to a part of it!
OTHELLO
How comes it, Michael, you are thus forgot?
CASSIO
I pray you, pardon me; I cannot speak.
OTHELLO
Worthy Montano, you were wont be civil;
The gravity and stillness of your youth
The world hath noted, and your name is great
In mouths of wisest censure: what's the matter,
That you unlace your reputation thus
And spend your rich opinion for the name
Of a night-brawler? give me answer to it.
MONTANO
Worthy Othello, I am hurt to danger:
Your officer, Iago, can inform you,--
While I spare speech, which something now
offends me,--
Of all that I do know: nor know I aught
By me that's said or done amiss this night;
Unless self-charity be sometimes a vice,
And to defend ourselves it be a sin
When violence assails us.
OTHELLO
Now, by heaven,
My blood begins my safer guides to rule;

And passion, having my best judgment collied,
Assays to lead the way: if I once stir,
Or do but lift this arm, the best of you
Shall sink in my rebuke. Give me to know
How this foul rout began, who set it on;
And he that is approved in this offence,
Though he had twinn'd with me, both at a birth,
Shall lose me. What! in a town of war,
Yet wild, the people's hearts brimful of fear,
To manage private and domestic quarrel,
In night, and on the court and guard of safety!
'Tis monstrous. Iago, who began't?

MONTANO

If partially affined, or leagued in office,
Thou dost deliver more or less than truth,
Thou art no soldier.

IAGO

Touch me not so near:
I had rather have this tongue cut from my mouth
Than it should do offence to Michael Cassio;
Yet, I persuade myself, to speak the truth
Shall nothing wrong him. Thus it is, general.
Montano and myself being in speech,
There comes a fellow crying out for help:
And Cassio following him with determined sword,
To execute upon him. Sir, this gentleman
Steps in to Cassio, and entreats his pause:
Myself the crying fellow did pursue,
Lest by his clamour--as it so fell out--
The town might fall in fright: he, swift of foot,
Outran my purpose; and I return'd the rather
For that I heard the clink and fall of swords,
And Cassio high in oath; which till to-night
I ne'er might say before. When I came back--

For this was brief--I found them close together,
At blow and thrust; even as again they were
When you yourself did part them.
More of this matter cannot I report:
But men are men; the best sometimes forget:
Though Cassio did some little wrong to him,
As men in rage strike those that wish them best,
Yet surely Cassio, I believe, received
From him that fled some strange indignity,
Which patience could not pass.
OTHELLO
I know, Iago,
Thy honesty and love doth mince this matter,
Making it light to Cassio. Cassio, I love thee
But never more be officer of mine.

Re-enter DESDEMONA, attended

Look, if my gentle love be not raised up!
I'll make thee an example.
DESDEMONA
What's the matter?
OTHELLO
All's well now, sweeting; come away to bed.
Sir, for your hurts, myself will be your surgeon:
Lead him off.

To MONTANO, who is led off

Iago, look with care about the town,
And silence those whom this vile brawl distracted.
Come, Desdemona: 'tis the soldiers' life
To have their balmy slumbers waked with strife.

Exeunt all but IAGO and CASSIO

IAGO

What, are you hurt, lieutenant?

CASSIO

Ay, past all surgery.

IAGO

Marry, heaven forbid!

CASSIO

Reputation, reputation, reputation! O, I have lost
my reputation! I have lost the immortal part of
myself, and what remains is bestial. My reputation,
Iago, my reputation!

IAGO

As I am an honest man, I thought you had received
some bodily wound; there is more sense in that than
in reputation. Reputation is an idle and most false
imposition: oft got without merit, and lost without
deserving: you have lost no reputation at all,
unless you repute yourself such a loser. What, man!
there are ways to recover the general again: you
are but now cast in his mood, a punishment more in
policy than in malice, even so as one would beat his
offenceless dog to affright an imperious lion: sue
to him again, and he's yours.

CASSIO

I will rather sue to be despised than to deceive so
good a commander with so slight, so drunken, and so
indiscreet an officer. Drunk? and speak parrot?
and squabble? swagger? swear? and discourse
fustian with one's own shadow? O thou invisible
spirit of wine, if thou hast no name to be known by,
let us call thee devil!

IAGO

What was he that you followed with your sword? What
had he done to you?

CASSIO
I know not.
IAGO
Is't possible?
CASSIO
I remember a mass of things, but nothing distinctly;
a quarrel, but nothing wherefore. O God, that men
should put an enemy in their mouths to steal away
their brains! that we should, with joy, pleasance
revel and applause, transform ourselves into beasts!
IAGO
Why, but you are now well enough: how came you thus
recovered?
CASSIO
It hath pleased the devil drunkenness to give place
to the devil wrath; one unperfectness shows me
another, to make me frankly despise myself.
IAGO
Come, you are too severe a moraler: as the time,
the place, and the condition of this country
stands, I could heartily wish this had not befallen;
but, since it is as it is, mend it for your own good.
CASSIO
I will ask him for my place again; he shall tell me
I am a drunkard! Had I as many mouths as Hydra,
such an answer would stop them all. To be now a
sensible man, by and by a fool, and presently a
beast! O strange! Every inordinate cup is
unblessed and the ingredient is a devil.
IAGO
Come, come, good wine is a good familiar creature,
if it be well used: exclaim no more against it.
And, good lieutenant, I think you think I love you.
CASSIO

I have well approved it, sir. I drunk!

IAGO

You or any man living may be drunk! at a time, man.
I'll tell you what you shall do. Our general's wife
is now the general: may say so in this respect, for
that he hath devoted and given up himself to the
contemplation, mark, and denotement of her parts and
graces: confess yourself freely to her; importune
her help to put you in your place again: she is of
so free, so kind, so apt, so blessed a disposition,
she holds it a vice in her goodness not to do more
than she is requested: this broken joint between
you and her husband entreat her to splinter; and, my
fortunes against any lay worth naming, this
crack of your love shall grow stronger than it was
before.

CASSIO

You advise me well.

IAGO

I protest, in the sincerity of love and honest kindness.

CASSIO

I think it freely; and betimes in the morning I will
beseech the virtuous Desdemona to undertake for me:
I am desperate of my fortunes if they cheque me here.

IAGO

You are in the right. Good night, lieutenant; I
must to the watch.

CASSIO: Good night, honest Iago.

Exit

IAGO

And what's he then that says I play the villain?
When this advice is free I give and honest,
Probal to thinking and indeed the course

To win the Moor again? For 'tis most easy
The inclining Desdemona to subdue
In any honest suit: she's framed as fruitful
As the free elements. And then for her
To win the Moor--were't to renounce his baptism,
All seals and symbols of redeemed sin,
His soul is so enfetter'd to her love,
That she may make, unmake, do what she list,
Even as her appetite shall play the god
With his weak function. How am I then a villain
To counsel Cassio to this parallel course,
Directly to his good? Divinity of hell!
When devils will the blackest sins put on,
They do suggest at first with heavenly shows,
As I do now: for whiles this honest fool
Plies Desdemona to repair his fortunes
And she for him pleads strongly to the Moor,
I'll pour this pestilence into his ear,
That she repeals him for her body's lust;
And by how much she strives to do him good,
She shall undo her credit with the Moor.
So will I turn her virtue into pitch,
And out of her own goodness make the net
That shall enmesh them all.

Re-enter RODERIGO

How now, Roderigo!
RODERIGO
I do follow here in the chase, not like a hound that
hunts, but one that fills up the cry. My money is
almost spent; I have been to-night exceedingly well
cudgelled; and I think the issue will be, I shall
have so much experience for my pains, and so, with

no money at all and a little more wit, return again to
Venice.

IAGO

How poor are they that have not patience!
What wound did ever heal but by degrees?
Thou know'st we work by wit, and not by witchcraft;
And wit depends on dilatory time.
Does't not go well? Cassio hath beaten thee.
And thou, by that small hurt, hast cashier'd Cassio:
Though other things grow fair against the sun,
Yet fruits that blossom first will first be ripe:
Content thyself awhile. By the mass, 'tis morning;
Pleasure and action make the hours seem short.
Retire thee; go where thou art billeted:
Away, I say; thou shalt know more hereafter:
Nay, get thee gone.

Exit RODERIGO

Two things are to be done:
My wife must move for Cassio to her mistress;
I'll set her on;
Myself the while to draw the Moor apart,
And bring him jump when he may Cassio find
Soliciting his wife: ay, that's the way
Dull not device by coldness and delay.

Exit

ACT III

SCENE I.

Before the castle.

Enter CASSIO and some Musicians

CASSIO
Masters, play here; I will content your pains;
Something that's brief; and bid 'Good morrow, general.'

Music

Enter Clown

Clown
Why masters, have your instruments been in Naples,
that they speak i' the nose thus?
First Musician
How, sir, how!
Clown
Are these, I pray you, wind-instruments?
First Musician
Ay, marry, are they, sir.
Clown
O, thereby hangs a tail.
First Musician
Whereby hangs a tale, sir?
Clown
Marry. sir, by many a wind-instrument that I know.
But, masters, here's money for you: and the general
so likes your music, that he desires you, for love's
sake, to make no more noise with it.
First Musician

Well, sir, we will not.

Clown

If you have any music that may not be heard, to't
again: but, as they say to hear music the general
does not greatly care.

First Musician

We have none such, sir.

Clown

Then put up your pipes in your bag, for I'll away:
go; vanish into air; away!

Exeunt Musicians

CASSIO

Dost thou hear, my honest friend?

Clown

No, I hear not your honest friend; I hear you.

CASSIO

Prithee, keep up thy quillets. There's a poor piece
of gold for thee: if the gentlewoman that attends
the general's wife be stirring, tell her there's
one Cassio entreats her a little favour of speech:
wilt thou do this?

Clown

She is stirring, sir: if she will stir hither, I
shall seem to notify unto her.

CASSIO

Do, good my friend.

Exit Clown

Enter IAGO

In happy time, Iago.

IAGO

You have not been a-bed, then?
CASSIO
    Why, no; the day had broke
    Before we parted. I have made bold, Iago,
    To send in to your wife: my suit to her
    Is, that she will to virtuous Desdemona
    Procure me some access.
IAGO
    I'll send her to you presently;
    And I'll devise a mean to draw the Moor
    Out of the way, that your converse and business
    May be more free.
CASSIO
    I humbly thank you for't.

Exit IAGO

    I never knew
    A Florentine more kind and honest.

Enter EMILIA

EMILIA
    Good morrow, good Lieutenant: I am sorry
    For your displeasure; but all will sure be well.
    The general and his wife are talking of it;
    And she speaks for you stoutly: the Moor replies,
    That he you hurt is of great fame in Cyprus,
    And great affinity, and that in wholesome wisdom
    He might not but refuse you; but he protests he loves
    you
    And needs no other suitor but his likings
    To take the safest occasion by the front
    To bring you in again.
CASSIO

Yet, I beseech you,
If you think fit, or that it may be done,
Give me advantage of some brief discourse
With Desdemona alone.

EMILIA

Pray you, come in;
I will bestow you where you shall have time
To speak your bosom freely.

CASSIO

I am much bound to you.

Exeunt

SCENE II.

A room in the castle.

Enter OTHELLO, IAGO, and Gentlemen

OTHELLO

These letters give, Iago, to the pilot;
And by him do my duties to the senate:
That done, I will be walking on the works;
Repair there to me.

IAGO

Well, my good lord, I'll do't.

OTHELLO

This fortification, gentlemen, shall we see't?

Gentleman

We'll wait upon your lordship.

Exeunt

SCENE III.

The garden of the castle.

Enter DESDEMONA, CASSIO, and EMILIA

DESDEMONA

Be thou assured, good Cassio, I will do
All my abilities in thy behalf.

EMILIA

Good madam, do: I warrant it grieves my husband,
As if the case were his.

DESDEMONA

O, that's an honest fellow. Do not doubt, Cassio,
But I will have my lord and you again
As friendly as you were.

CASSIO

Bounteous madam,
Whatever shall become of Michael Cassio,
He's never any thing but your true servant.

DESDEMONA

I know't; I thank you. You do love my lord:
You have known him long; and be you well assured
He shall in strangeness stand no further off
Than in a polite distance.

CASSIO

Ay, but, lady,
That policy may either last so long,
Or feed upon such nice and waterish diet,
Or breed itself so out of circumstance,
That, I being absent and my place supplied,
My general will forget my love and service.

DESDEMONA

Do not doubt that; before Emilia here
I give thee warrant of thy place: assure thee,
If I do vow a friendship, I'll perform it

To the last article: my lord shall never rest;
I'll watch him tame and talk him out of patience;
His bed shall seem a school, his board a shrift;
I'll intermingle every thing he does
With Cassio's suit: therefore be merry, Cassio;
For thy solicitor shall rather die
Than give thy cause away.

EMILIA

Madam, here comes my lord.

CASSIO

Madam, I'll take my leave.

DESDEMONA

Why, stay, and hear me speak.

CASSIO

Madam, not now: I am very ill at ease,
Unfit for mine own purposes.

DESDEMONA

Well, do your discretion.

Exit CASSIO

Enter OTHELLO and IAGO

IAGO

Ha! I like not that.

OTHELLO

What dost thou say?

IAGO

Nothing, my lord: or if--I know not what.

OTHELLO

Was not that Cassio parted from my wife?

IAGO

Cassio, my lord! No, sure, I cannot think it,
That he would steal away so guilty-like,

Seeing you coming.
OTHELLO
I do believe 'twas he.
DESDEMONA
How now, my lord!
I have been talking with a suitor here,
A man that languishes in your displeasure.
OTHELLO
Who is't you mean?
DESDEMONA
Why, your lieutenant, Cassio. Good my lord,
If I have any grace or power to move you,
His present reconciliation take;
For if he be not one that truly loves you,
That errs in ignorance and not in cunning,
I have no judgment in an honest face:
I prithee, call him back.
OTHELLO
Went he hence now?
DESDEMONA
Ay, sooth; so humbled
That he hath left part of his grief with me,
To suffer with him. Good love, call him back.
OTHELLO
Not now, sweet Desdemona; some other time.
DESDEMONA
But shall't be shortly?
OTHELLO
The sooner, sweet, for you.
DESDEMONA
Shall't be to-night at supper?
OTHELLO
No, not to-night.
DESDEMONA

To-morrow dinner, then?

OTHELLO

I shall not dine at home;
I meet the captains at the citadel.

DESDEMONA

Why, then, to-morrow night; or Tuesday morn;
On Tuesday noon, or night; on Wednesday morn:
I prithee, name the time, but let it not
Exceed three days: in faith, he's penitent;
And yet his trespass, in our common reason--
Save that, they say, the wars must make examples
Out of their best--is not almost a fault
To incur a private cheque. When shall he come?
Tell me, Othello: I wonder in my soul,
What you would ask me, that I should deny,
Or stand so mammering on. What! Michael Cassio,
That came a-wooing with you, and so many a time,
When I have spoke of you dispraisingly,
Hath ta'en your part; to have so much to do
To bring him in! Trust me, I could do much,--

OTHELLO

Prithee, no more: let him come when he will;
I will deny thee nothing.

DESDEMONA

Why, this is not a boon;
'Tis as I should entreat you wear your gloves,
Or feed on nourishing dishes, or keep you warm,
Or sue to you to do a peculiar profit
To your own person: nay, when I have a suit
Wherein I mean to touch your love indeed,
It shall be full of poise and difficult weight
And fearful to be granted.

OTHELLO

I will deny thee nothing:

Whereon, I do beseech thee, grant me this,
To leave me but a little to myself.

DESDEMONA

Shall I deny you? no: farewell, my lord.

OTHELLO

Farewell, my Desdemona: I'll come to thee straight.

DESDEMONA

Emilia, come. Be as your fancies teach you;
Whate'er you be, I am obedient.

Exeunt DESDEMONA and EMILIA

OTHELLO

Excellent wretch! Perdition catch my soul,
But I do love thee! and when I love thee not,
Chaos is come again.

IAGO

My noble lord--

OTHELLO

What dost thou say, Iago?

IAGO

Did Michael Cassio, when you woo'd my lady,
Know of your love?

OTHELLO

He did, from first to last: why dost thou ask?

IAGO

But for a satisfaction of my thought;
No further harm.

OTHELLO

Why of thy thought, Iago?

IAGO

I did not think he had been acquainted with her.

OTHELLO

O, yes; and went between us very oft.

IAGO

Indeed!
OTHELLO
  Indeed! ay, indeed: discern'st thou aught in that?
  Is he not honest?
IAGO
  Honest, my lord!
OTHELLO
  Honest! ay, honest.
IAGO
  My lord, for aught I know.
OTHELLO
  What dost thou think?
IAGO
  Think, my lord!
OTHELLO
  Think, my lord!
  By heaven, he echoes me,
  As if there were some monster in his thought
  Too hideous to be shown. Thou dost mean something:
  I heard thee say even now, thou likedst not that,
  When Cassio left my wife: what didst not like?
  And when I told thee he was of my counsel
  In my whole course of wooing, thou criedst 'Indeed!'
  And didst contract and purse thy brow together,
  As if thou then hadst shut up in thy brain
  Some horrible conceit: if thou dost love me,
  Show me thy thought.
IAGO
  My lord, you know I love you.
OTHELLO
  I think thou dost;
  And, for I know thou'rt full of love and honesty,
  And weigh'st thy words before thou givest them breath,
  Therefore these stops of thine fright me the more:

For such things in a false disloyal knave
Are tricks of custom, but in a man that's just
They are close delations, working from the heart
That passion cannot rule.
IAGO
For Michael Cassio,
I dare be sworn I think that he is honest.
OTHELLO
I think so too.
IAGO
Men should be what they seem;
Or those that be not, would they might seem none!
OTHELLO
Certain, men should be what they seem.
IAGO
Why, then, I think Cassio's an honest man.
OTHELLO
Nay, yet there's more in this:
I prithee, speak to me as to thy thinkings,
As thou dost ruminate, and give thy worst of thoughts
The worst of words.
IAGO
Good my lord, pardon me:
Though I am bound to every act of duty,
I am not bound to that all slaves are free to.
Utter my thoughts? Why, say they are vile and false;
As where's that palace whereinto foul things
Sometimes intrude not? who has a breast so pure,
But some uncleanly apprehensions
Keep leets and law-days and in session sit
With meditations lawful?
OTHELLO
Thou dost conspire against thy friend, Iago,
If thou but think'st him wrong'd and makest his ear

A stranger to thy thoughts.
IAGO
   I do beseech you--
   Though I perchance am vicious in my guess,
   As, I confess, it is my nature's plague
   To spy into abuses, and oft my jealousy
   Shapes faults that are not--that your wisdom yet,
   From one that so imperfectly conceits,
   Would take no notice, nor build yourself a trouble
   Out of his scattering and unsure observance.
   It were not for your quiet nor your good,
   Nor for my manhood, honesty, or wisdom,
   To let you know my thoughts.
OTHELLO
   What dost thou mean?
IAGO
   Good name in man and woman, dear my lord,
   Is the immediate jewel of their souls:
   Who steals my purse steals trash; 'tis something,
   nothing;
   'Twas mine, 'tis his, and has been slave to thousands:
   But he that filches from me my good name
   Robs me of that which not enriches him
   And makes me poor indeed.
OTHELLO
   By heaven, I'll know thy thoughts.
IAGO
   You cannot, if my heart were in your hand;
   Nor shall not, whilst 'tis in my custody.
OTHELLO
   Ha!
IAGO
   O, beware, my lord, of jealousy;
   It is the green-eyed monster which doth mock

The meat it feeds on; that cuckold lives in bliss
Who, certain of his fate, loves not his wronger;
But, O, what damned minutes tells he o'er
Who dotes, yet doubts, suspects, yet strongly loves!

OTHELLO

O misery!

IAGO

Poor and content is rich and rich enough,
But riches fineless is as poor as winter
To him that ever fears he shall be poor.
Good heaven, the souls of all my tribe defend
From jealousy!

OTHELLO

Why, why is this?
Think'st thou I'ld make a lie of jealousy,
To follow still the changes of the moon
With fresh suspicions? No; to be once in doubt
Is once to be resolved: exchange me for a goat,
When I shall turn the business of my soul
To such exsufflicate and blown surmises,
Matching thy inference. 'Tis not to make me jealous
To say my wife is fair, feeds well, loves company,
Is free of speech, sings, plays and dances well;
Where virtue is, these are more virtuous:
Nor from mine own weak merits will I draw
The smallest fear or doubt of her revolt;
For she had eyes, and chose me. No, Iago;
I'll see before I doubt; when I doubt, prove;
And on the proof, there is no more but this,--
Away at once with love or jealousy!

IAGO

I am glad of it; for now I shall have reason
To show the love and duty that I bear you
With franker spirit: therefore, as I am bound,

Receive it from me. I speak not yet of proof.
Look to your wife; observe her well with Cassio;
Wear your eye thus, not jealous nor secure:
I would not have your free and noble nature,
Out of self-bounty, be abused; look to't:
I know our country disposition well;
In Venice they do let heaven see the pranks
They dare not show their husbands; their best
conscience
Is not to leave't undone, but keep't unknown.

OTHELLO

Dost thou say so?

IAGO

She did deceive her father, marrying you;
And when she seem'd to shake and fear your looks,
She loved them most.

OTHELLO

And so she did.

IAGO

Why, go to then;
She that, so young, could give out such a seeming,
To seal her father's eyes up close as oak-
He thought 'twas witchcraft--but I am much to blame;
I humbly do beseech you of your pardon
For too much loving you.

OTHELLO

I am bound to thee for ever.

IAGO

I see this hath a little dash'd your spirits.

OTHELLO

Not a jot, not a jot.

IAGO

I' faith, I fear it has.
I hope you will consider what is spoke

Comes from my love. But I do see you're moved:
I am to pray you not to strain my speech
To grosser issues nor to larger reach
Than to suspicion.

OTHELLO

I will not.

IAGO

Should you do so, my lord,
My speech should fall into such vile success
As my thoughts aim not at. Cassio's my worthy friend--
My lord, I see you're moved.

OTHELLO

No, not much moved:
I do not think but Desdemona's honest.

IAGO

Long live she so! and long live you to think so!

OTHELLO

And yet, how nature erring from itself,--

IAGO

Ay, there's the point: as--to be bold with you--
Not to affect many proposed matches
Of her own clime, complexion, and degree,
Whereto we see in all things nature tends--
Foh! one may smell in such a will most rank,
Foul disproportion thoughts unnatural.
But pardon me; I do not in position
Distinctly speak of her; though I may fear
Her will, recoiling to her better judgment,
May fall to match you with her country forms
And happily repent.

OTHELLO

Farewell, farewell:
If more thou dost perceive, let me know more;
Set on thy wife to observe: leave me, Iago:

IAGO

[Going] My lord, I take my leave.

OTHELLO

Why did I marry? This honest creature doubtless

Sees and knows more, much more, than he unfolds.

IAGO

[Returning] My lord, I would I might entreat

your honour

To scan this thing no further; leave it to time:

Though it be fit that Cassio have his place,

For sure, he fills it up with great ability,

Yet, if you please to hold him off awhile,

You shall by that perceive him and his means:

Note, if your lady strain his entertainment

With any strong or vehement importunity;

Much will be seen in that. In the mean time,

Let me be thought too busy in my fears--

As worthy cause I have to fear I am--

And hold her free, I do beseech your honour.

OTHELLO

Fear not my government.

IAGO

I once more take my leave.

Exit

OTHELLO

This fellow's of exceeding honesty,

And knows all qualities, with a learned spirit,

Of human dealings. If I do prove her haggard,

Though that her jesses were my dear heartstrings,

I'ld whistle her off and let her down the wind,

To pray at fortune. Haply, for I am black

And have not those soft parts of conversation

That chamberers have, or for I am declined

Into the vale of years,--yet that's not much--
She's gone. I am abused; and my relief
Must be to loathe her. O curse of marriage,
That we can call these delicate creatures ours,
And not their appetites! I had rather be a toad,
And live upon the vapour of a dungeon,
Than keep a corner in the thing I love
For others' uses. Yet, 'tis the plague of great ones;
Prerogatived are they less than the base;
'Tis destiny unshunnable, like death:
Even then this forked plague is fated to us
When we do quicken. Desdemona comes:

Re-enter DESDEMONA and EMILIA

If she be false, O, then heaven mocks itself!
I'll not believe't.
DESDEMONA
How now, my dear Othello!
Your dinner, and the generous islanders
By you invited, do attend your presence.
OTHELLO
I am to blame.
DESDEMONA
Why do you speak so faintly?
Are you not well?
OTHELLO
I have a pain upon my forehead here.
DESDEMONA
'Faith, that's with watching; 'twill away again:
Let me but bind it hard, within this hour
It will be well.
OTHELLO
Your napkin is too little:
He puts the handkerchief from him; and it drops

Let it alone. Come, I'll go in with you.
DESDEMONA

I am very sorry that you are not well.

Exeunt OTHELLO and DESDEMONA

EMILIA

I am glad I have found this napkin:
This was her first remembrance from the Moor:
My wayward husband hath a hundred times
Woo'd me to steal it; but she so loves the token,
For he conjured her she should ever keep it,
That she reserves it evermore about her
To kiss and talk to. I'll have the work ta'en out,
And give't Iago: what he will do with it
Heaven knows, not I;
I nothing but to please his fantasy.

Re-enter Iago

IAGO

How now! what do you here alone?
EMILIA

Do not you chide; I have a thing for you.
IAGO

A thing for me? it is a common thing--
EMILIA

Ha!
IAGO

To have a foolish wife.
EMILIA

O, is that all? What will you give me now
For the same handkerchief?
IAGO

What handkerchief?
EMILIA
What handkerchief?
Why, that the Moor first gave to Desdemona;
That which so often you did bid me steal.
IAGO
Hast stol'n it from her?
EMILIA
No, 'faith; she let it drop by negligence.
And, to the advantage, I, being here, took't up.
Look, here it is.
IAGO
A good wench; give it me.
EMILIA
What will you do with 't, that you have been
so earnest
To have me filch it?
IAGO
[Snatching it] Why, what's that to you?
EMILIA
If it be not for some purpose of import,
Give't me again: poor lady, she'll run mad
When she shall lack it.
IAGO
Be not acknown on 't; I have use for it.
Go, leave me.

Exit EMILIA

I will in Cassio's lodging lose this napkin,
And let him find it. Trifles light as air
Are to the jealous confirmations strong
As proofs of holy writ: this may do something.
The Moor already changes with my poison:
Dangerous conceits are, in their natures, poisons.

Which at the first are scarce found to distaste,
But with a little act upon the blood.
Burn like the mines of Sulphur. I did say so:
Look, where he comes!

Re-enter OTHELLO

Not poppy, nor mandragora,
Nor all the drowsy syrups of the world,
Shall ever medicine thee to that sweet sleep
Which thou owedst yesterday.

OTHELLO

Ha! ha! false to me?

IAGO

Why, how now, general! no more of that.

OTHELLO

Avaunt! be gone! thou hast set me on the rack:
I swear 'tis better to be much abused
Than but to know't a little.

IAGO

How now, my lord!

OTHELLO

What sense had I of her stol'n hours of lust?
I saw't not, thought it not, it harm'd not me:
I slept the next night well, was free and merry;
I found not Cassio's kisses on her lips:
He that is robb'd, not wanting what is stol'n,
Let him not know't, and he's not robb'd at all.

IAGO

I am sorry to hear this.

OTHELLO

I had been happy, if the general camp,
Pioners and all, had tasted her sweet body,
So I had nothing known. O, now, for ever
Farewell the tranquil mind! farewell content!

Farewell the plumed troop, and the big wars,
That make ambition virtue! O, farewell!
Farewell the neighing steed, and the shrill trump,
The spirit-stirring drum, the ear-piercing fife,
The royal banner, and all quality,
Pride, pomp and circumstance of glorious war!
And, O you mortal engines, whose rude throats
The immortal Jove's dead clamours counterfeit,
Farewell! Othello's occupation's gone!

IAGO

Is't possible, my lord?

OTHELLO

Villain, be sure thou prove my love a whore,
Be sure of it; give me the ocular proof:
Or by the worth of man's eternal soul,
Thou hadst been better have been born a dog
Than answer my waked wrath!

IAGO

Is't come to this?

OTHELLO

Make me to see't; or, at the least, so prove it,
That the probation bear no hinge nor loop
To hang a doubt on; or woe upon thy life!

IAGO

My noble lord,--

OTHELLO

If thou dost slander her and torture me,
Never pray more; abandon all remorse;
On horror's head horrors accumulate;
Do deeds to make heaven weep, all earth amazed;
For nothing canst thou to damnation add
Greater than that.

IAGO

O grace! O heaven forgive me!

Are you a man? have you a soul or sense?
God be wi' you; take mine office. O wretched fool.
That livest to make thine honesty a vice!
O monstrous world! Take note, take note, O world,
To be direct and honest is not safe.
I thank you for this profit; and from hence
I'll love no friend, sith love breeds such offence.

OTHELLO

Nay, stay: thou shouldst be honest.

IAGO

I should be wise, for honesty's a fool
And loses that it works for.

OTHELLO

By the world,
I think my wife be honest and think she is not;
I think that thou art just and think thou art not.
I'll have some proof. Her name, that was as fresh
As Dian's visage, is now begrimed and black
As mine own face. If there be cords, or knives,
Poison, or fire, or suffocating streams,
I'll not endure it. Would I were satisfied!

IAGO

I see, sir, you are eaten up with passion:
I do repent me that I put it to you.
You would be satisfied?

OTHELLO

Would! nay, I will.

IAGO

And may: but, how? how satisfied, my lord?
Would you, the supervisor, grossly gape on--
Behold her topp'd?

OTHELLO

Death and damnation! O!

IAGO

It were a tedious difficulty, I think,
To bring them to that prospect: damn them then,
If ever mortal eyes do see them bolster
More than their own! What then? how then?
What shall I say? Where's satisfaction?
It is impossible you should see this,
Were they as prime as goats, as hot as monkeys,
As salt as wolves in pride, and fools as gross
As ignorance made drunk. But yet, I say,
If imputation and strong circumstances,
Which lead directly to the door of truth,
Will give you satisfaction, you may have't.

OTHELLO

Give me a living reason she's disloyal.

IAGO

I do not like the office:
But, sith I am enter'd in this cause so far,
Prick'd to't by foolish honesty and love,
I will go on. I lay with Cassio lately;
And, being troubled with a raging tooth,
I could not sleep.
There are a kind of men so loose of soul,
That in their sleeps will mutter their affairs:
One of this kind is Cassio:
In sleep I heard him say 'Sweet Desdemona,
Let us be wary, let us hide our loves;'
And then, sir, would he gripe and wring my hand,
Cry 'O sweet creature!' and then kiss me hard,
As if he pluck'd up kisses by the roots
That grew upon my lips: then laid his leg
Over my thigh, and sigh'd, and kiss'd; and then
Cried 'Cursed fate that gave thee to the Moor!'

OTHELLO

O monstrous! monstrous!

IAGO

Nay, this was but his dream.

OTHELLO

But this denoted a foregone conclusion:

'Tis a shrewd doubt, though it be but a dream.

IAGO

And this may help to thicken other proofs

That do demonstrate thinly.

OTHELLO

I'll tear her all to pieces.

IAGO

Nay, but be wise: yet we see nothing done;

She may be honest yet. Tell me but this,

Have you not sometimes seen a handkerchief

Spotted with strawberries in your wife's hand?

OTHELLO

I gave her such a one; 'twas my first gift.

IAGO

I know not that; but such a handkerchief--

I am sure it was your wife's--did I to-day

See Cassio wipe his beard with.

OTHELLO

If it be that--

IAGO

If it be that, or any that was hers,

It speaks against her with the other proofs.

OTHELLO

O, that the slave had forty thousand lives!

One is too poor, too weak for my revenge.

Now do I see 'tis true. Look here, Iago;

All my fond love thus do I blow to heaven.

'Tis gone.

Arise, black vengeance, from thy hollow cell!

Yield up, O love, thy crown and hearted throne

To tyrannous hate! Swell, bosom, with thy fraught,
For 'tis of aspics' tongues!

IAGO

Yet be content.

OTHELLO

O, blood, blood, blood!

IAGO

Patience, I say; your mind perhaps may change.

OTHELLO

Never, Iago: Like to the Pontic sea,
Whose icy current and compulsive course
Ne'er feels retiring ebb, but keeps due on
To the Propontic and the Hellespont,
Even so my bloody thoughts, with violent pace,
Shall ne'er look back, ne'er ebb to humble love,
Till that a capable and wide revenge
Swallow them up. Now, by yond marble heaven,

Kneels

In the due reverence of a sacred vow
I here engage my words.

IAGO

Do not rise yet.

Kneels

Witness, you ever-burning lights above,
You elements that clip us round about,
Witness that here Iago doth give up
The execution of his wit, hands, heart,
To wrong'd Othello's service! Let him command,
And to obey shall be in me remorse,
What bloody business ever.

They rise

OTHELLO

    I greet thy love,

    Not with vain thanks, but with acceptance bounteous,

    And will upon the instant put thee to't:

    Within these three days let me hear thee say

    That Cassio's not alive.

IAGO

    My friend is dead; 'tis done at your request:

    But let her live.

OTHELLO

    Damn her, lewd minx! O, damn her!

    Come, go with me apart; I will withdraw,

    To furnish me with some swift means of death

    For the fair devil. Now art thou my lieutenant.

IAGO

    I am your own for ever.

Exeunt

SCENE IV.

Before the castle.

Enter DESDEMONA, EMILIA, and Clown

DESDEMONA

    Do you know, sirrah, where Lieutenant Cassio lies?

Clown

    I dare not say he lies any where.

DESDEMONA

    Why, man?

Clown

    He's a soldier, and for one to say a soldier lies,

    is stabbing.

DESDEMONA

Go to: where lodges he?
Clown

To tell you where he lodges, is to tell you where I lie.
DESDEMONA

Can any thing be made of this?
Clown

I know not where he lodges, and for me to devise a
lodging and say he lies here or he lies there, were
to lie in mine own throat.
DESDEMONA

Can you inquire him out, and be edified by report?
Clown

I will catechise the world for him; that is, make
questions, and by them answer.
DESDEMONA

Seek him, bid him come hither: tell him I have
moved my lord on his behalf, and hope all will be well.
Clown

To do this is within the compass of man's wit: and
therefore I will attempt the doing it.

Exit

DESDEMONA

Where should I lose that handkerchief, Emilia?
EMILIA

I know not, madam.
DESDEMONA

Believe me, I had rather have lost my purse
Full of crusadoes: and, but my noble Moor
Is true of mind and made of no such baseness
As jealous creatures are, it were enough
To put him to ill thinking.
EMILIA

Is he not jealous?

DESDEMONA
  Who, he? I think the sun where he was born
  Drew all such humours from him.
EMILIA
  Look, where he comes.
DESDEMONA
  I will not leave him now till Cassio
  Be call'd to him.

Enter OTHELLO

  How is't with you, my lord
OTHELLO
  Well, my good lady.

Aside

  O, hardness to dissemble!--
  How do you, Desdemona?
DESDEMONA
  Well, my good lord.
OTHELLO
  Give me your hand: this hand is moist, my lady.
DESDEMONA
  It yet hath felt no age nor known no sorrow.
OTHELLO
  This argues fruitfulness and liberal heart:
  Hot, hot, and moist: this hand of yours requires
  A sequester from liberty, fasting and prayer,
  Much castigation, exercise devout;
  For here's a young and sweating devil here,
  That commonly rebels. 'Tis a good hand,
  A frank one.
DESDEMONA
  You may, indeed, say so;

For 'twas that hand that gave away my heart.

OTHELLO

A liberal hand: the hearts of old gave hands;
But our new heraldry is hands, not hearts.

DESDEMONA

I cannot speak of this. Come now, your promise.

OTHELLO

What promise, chuck?

DESDEMONA

I have sent to bid Cassio come speak with you.

OTHELLO

I have a salt and sorry rheum offends me;
Lend me thy handkerchief.

DESDEMONA

Here, my lord.

OTHELLO

That which I gave you.

DESDEMONA

I have it not about me.

OTHELLO

Not?

DESDEMONA

No, indeed, my lord.

OTHELLO

That is a fault.
That handkerchief
Did an Egyptian to my mother give;
She was a charmer, and could almost read
The thoughts of people: she told her, while
she kept it,
'Twould make her amiable and subdue my father
Entirely to her love, but if she lost it
Or made gift of it, my father's eye
Should hold her loathed and his spirits should hunt

After new fancies: she, dying, gave it me;
And bid me, when my fate would have me wive,
To give it her. I did so: and take heed on't;
Make it a darling like your precious eye;
To lose't or give't away were such perdition
As nothing else could match.

DESDEMONA

Is't possible?

OTHELLO

'Tis true: there's magic in the web of it:
A sibyl, that had number'd in the world
The sun to course two hundred compasses,
In her prophetic fury sew'd the work;
The worms were hallow'd that did breed the silk;
And it was dyed in mummy which the skilful
Conserved of maidens' hearts.

DESDEMONA

Indeed! is't true?

OTHELLO

Most veritable; therefore look to't well.

DESDEMONA

Then would to God that I had never seen't!

OTHELLO

Ha! wherefore?

DESDEMONA

Why do you speak so startingly and rash?

OTHELLO

Is't lost? is't gone? speak, is it out
o' the way?

DESDEMONA

Heaven bless us!

OTHELLO

Say you?

DESDEMONA

It is not lost; but what an if it were?
OTHELLO
  How!
DESDEMONA
  I say, it is not lost.
OTHELLO
  Fetch't, let me see't.
DESDEMONA
  Why, so I can, sir, but I will not now.
  This is a trick to put me from my suit:
  Pray you, let Cassio be received again.
OTHELLO
  Fetch me the handkerchief: my mind misgives.
DESDEMONA
  Come, come;
  You'll never meet a more sufficient man.
OTHELLO
  The handkerchief!
DESDEMONA
  I pray, talk me of Cassio.
OTHELLO
  The handkerchief!
DESDEMONA
  A man that all his time
  Hath founded his good fortunes on your love,
  Shared dangers with you,--
OTHELLO
  The handkerchief!
DESDEMONA
  In sooth, you are to blame.
OTHELLO
  Away!

Exit

EMILIA

Is not this man jealous?

DESDEMONA

I ne'er saw this before.

Sure, there's some wonder in this handkerchief:

I am most unhappy in the loss of it.

EMILIA

'Tis not a year or two shows us a man:

They are all but stomachs, and we all but food;

To eat us hungerly, and when they are full,

They belch us. Look you, Cassio and my husband!

Enter CASSIO and IAGO

IAGO

There is no other way; 'tis she must do't:

And, lo, the happiness! go, and importune her.

DESDEMONA

How now, good Cassio! what's the news with you?

CASSIO

Madam, my former suit: I do beseech you

That by your virtuous means I may again

Exist, and be a member of his love

Whom I with all the office of my heart

Entirely honour: I would not be delay'd.

If my offence be of such mortal kind

That nor my service past, nor present sorrows,

Nor purposed merit in futurity,

Can ransom me into his love again,

But to know so must be my benefit;

So shall I clothe me in a forced content,

And shut myself up in some other course,

To fortune's alms.

DESDEMONA

Alas, thrice-gentle Cassio!

My advocation is not now in tune;
My lord is not my lord; nor should I know him,
Were he in favour as in humour alter'd.
So help me every spirit sanctified,
As I have spoken for you all my best
And stood within the blank of his displeasure
For my free speech! you must awhile be patient:
What I can do I will; and more I will
Than for myself I dare: let that suffice you.

IAGO

Is my lord angry?

EMILIA

He went hence but now,
And certainly in strange unquietness.

IAGO

Can he be angry? I have seen the cannon,
When it hath blown his ranks into the air,
And, like the devil, from his very arm
Puff'd his own brother:--and can he be angry?
Something of moment then: I will go meet him:
There's matter in't indeed, if he be angry.

DESDEMONA

I prithee, do so.

Exit IAGO

Something, sure, of state,
Either from Venice, or some unhatch'd practise
Made demonstrable here in Cyprus to him,
Hath puddled his clear spirit: and in such cases
Men's natures wrangle with inferior things,
Though great ones are their object. 'Tis even so;
For let our finger ache, and it indues
Our other healthful members even to that sense
Of pain: nay, we must think men are not gods,

Nor of them look for such observances
As fit the bridal. Beshrew me much, Emilia,
I was, unhandsome warrior as I am,
Arraigning his unkindness with my soul;
But now I find I had suborn'd the witness,
And he's indicted falsely.

EMILIA

Pray heaven it be state-matters, as you think,
And no conception nor no jealous toy
Concerning you.

DESDEMONA

Alas the day! I never gave him cause.

EMILIA

But jealous souls will not be answer'd so;
They are not ever jealous for the cause,
But jealous for they are jealous: 'tis a monster
Begot upon itself, born on itself.

DESDEMONA

Heaven keep that monster from Othello's mind!

EMILIA

Lady, amen.

DESDEMONA

I will go seek him. Cassio, walk hereabout:
If I do find him fit, I'll move your suit
And seek to effect it to my uttermost.

CASSIO

I humbly thank your ladyship.

Exeunt DESDEMONA and EMILIA

Enter BIANCA

BIANCA

Save you, friend Cassio!

CASSIO
What make you from home?
How is it with you, my most fair Bianca?
I' faith, sweet love, I was coming to your house.
BIANCA
And I was going to your lodging, Cassio.
What, keep a week away? seven days and nights?
Eight score eight hours? and lovers' absent hours,
More tedious than the dial eight score times?
O weary reckoning!
CASSIO
Pardon me, Bianca:
I have this while with leaden thoughts been press'd:
But I shall, in a more continuate time,
Strike off this score of absence. Sweet Bianca,

Giving her DESDEMONA's handkerchief

Take me this work out.
BIANCA
O Cassio, whence came this?
This is some token from a newer friend:
To the felt absence now I feel a cause:
Is't come to this? Well, well.
CASSIO
Go to, woman!
Throw your vile guesses in the devil's teeth,
From whence you have them. You are jealous now
That this is from some mistress, some remembrance:
No, in good troth, Bianca.
BIANCA
Why, whose is it?
CASSIO
I know not, sweet: I found it in my chamber.
I like the work well: ere it be demanded--

As like enough it will--I'ld have it copied:
Take it, and do't; and leave me for this time.
BIANCA
Leave you! wherefore?
CASSIO
I do attend here on the general;
And think it no addition, nor my wish,
To have him see me woman'd.
BIANCA
Why, I pray you?
CASSIO
Not that I love you not.
BIANCA
But that you do not love me.
I pray you, bring me on the way a little,
And say if I shall see you soon at night.
CASSIO
'Tis but a little way that I can bring you;
For I attend here: but I'll see you soon.
BIANCA
'Tis very good; I must be circumstanced.

Exeunt

ACT IV

SCENE I.

Cyprus. Before the castle.

Enter OTHELLO and IAGO

IAGO
    Will you think so?
OTHELLO
    Think so, Iago!
IAGO
    What,
    To kiss in private?
OTHELLO
    An unauthorized kiss.
IAGO
    Or to be naked with her friend in bed
    An hour or more, not meaning any harm?
OTHELLO
    Naked in bed, Iago, and not mean harm!
    It is hypocrisy against the devil:
    They that mean virtuously, and yet do so,
    The devil their virtue tempts, and they tempt heaven.
IAGO
    So they do nothing, 'tis a venial slip:
    But if I give my wife a handkerchief,--
OTHELLO
    What then?
IAGO
    Why, then, 'tis hers, my lord; and, being hers,
    She may, I think, bestow't on any man.
OTHELLO
    She is protectress of her honour too:

May she give that?

IAGO

Her honour is an essence that's not seen;
They have it very oft that have it not:
But, for the handkerchief,--

OTHELLO

By heaven, I would most gladly have forgot it.
Thou said'st, it comes o'er my memory,
As doth the raven o'er the infected house,
Boding to all--he had my handkerchief.

IAGO

Ay, what of that?

OTHELLO

That's not so good now.

IAGO

What,
If I had said I had seen him do you wrong?
Or heard him say,--as knaves be such abroad,
Who having, by their own importunate suit,
Or voluntary dotage of some mistress,
Convinced or supplied them, cannot choose
But they must blab--

OTHELLO

Hath he said any thing?

IAGO

He hath, my lord; but be you well assured,
No more than he'll unswear.

OTHELLO

What hath he said?

IAGO

'Faith, that he did--I know not what he did.

OTHELLO

What? what?

IAGO

Lie--
OTHELLO
  With her?
IAGO
  With her, on her; what you will.
OTHELLO
  Lie with her! lie on her! We say lie on her, when
  they belie her. Lie with her! that's fulsome.
  --Handkerchief--confessions--handkerchief!--To
  confess, and be hanged for his labour;--first, to be
  hanged, and then to confess.--I tremble at it.
  Nature would not invest herself in such shadowing
  passion without some instruction. It is not words
  that shake me thus. Pish! Noses, ears, and lips.
  --Is't possible?--Confess--handkerchief!--O devil!--

Falls in a trance

IAGO
  Work on,
  My medicine, work! Thus credulous fools are caught;
  And many worthy and chaste dames even thus,
  All guiltless, meet reproach. What, ho! my lord!
  My lord, I say! Othello!

Enter CASSIO

  How now, Cassio!
CASSIO
  What's the matter?
IAGO
  My lord is fall'n into an epilepsy:
  This is his second fit; he had one yesterday.
CASSIO
  Rub him about the temples.

IAGO

No, forbear;
The lethargy must have his quiet course:
If not, he foams at mouth and by and by
Breaks out to savage madness. Look he stirs:
Do you withdraw yourself a little while,
He will recover straight: when he is gone,
I would on great occasion speak with you.

Exit CASSIO

How is it, general? have you not hurt your head?

OTHELLO

Dost thou mock me?

IAGO

I mock you! no, by heaven.
Would you would bear your fortune like a man!

OTHELLO

A horned man's a monster and a beast.

IAGO

There's many a beast then in a populous city,
And many a civil monster.

OTHELLO

Did he confess it?

IAGO

Good sir, be a man;
Think every bearded fellow that's but yoked
May draw with you: there's millions now alive
That nightly lie in those unproper beds
Which they dare swear peculiar: your case is better.
O, 'tis the spite of hell, the fiend's arch-mock,
To lip a wanton in a secure couch,
And to suppose her chaste! No, let me know;
And knowing what I am, I know what she shall be.

OTHELLO

O, thou art wise; 'tis certain.

IAGO

    Stand you awhile apart;
    Confine yourself but in a patient list.
    Whilst you were here o'erwhelmed with your grief--
    A passion most unsuiting such a man--
    Cassio came hither: I shifted him away,
    And laid good 'scuse upon your ecstasy,
    Bade him anon return and here speak with me;
    The which he promised. Do but encave yourself,
    And mark the fleers, the gibes, and notable scorns,
    That dwell in every region of his face;
    For I will make him tell the tale anew,
    Where, how, how oft, how long ago, and when
    He hath, and is again to cope your wife:
    I say, but mark his gesture. Marry, patience;
    Or I shall say you are all in all in spleen,
    And nothing of a man.

OTHELLO

    Dost thou hear, Iago?
    I will be found most cunning in my patience;
    But--dost thou hear?--most bloody.

IAGO

    That's not amiss;
    But yet keep time in all. Will you withdraw?

OTHELLO retires

    Now will I question Cassio of Bianca,
    A housewife that by selling her desires
    Buys herself bread and clothes: it is a creature
    That dotes on Cassio; as 'tis the strumpet's plague
    To beguile many and be beguiled by one:
    He, when he hears of her, cannot refrain
    From the excess of laughter. Here he comes:

Re-enter CASSIO

As he shall smile, Othello shall go mad;
And his unbookish jealousy must construe
Poor Cassio's smiles, gestures and light behavior,
Quite in the wrong. How do you now, lieutenant?
CASSIO
The worser that you give me the addition
Whose want even kills me.
IAGO
Ply Desdemona well, and you are sure on't.

Speaking lower

Now, if this suit lay in Bianco's power,
How quickly should you speed!
CASSIO
Alas, poor caitiff!
OTHELLO
Look, how he laughs already!
IAGO
I never knew woman love man so.
CASSIO
Alas, poor rogue! I think, i' faith, she loves me.
OTHELLO
Now he denies it faintly, and laughs it out.
IAGO
Do you hear, Cassio?
OTHELLO
Now he importunes him
To tell it o'er: go to; well said, well said.
IAGO
She gives it out that you shall marry hey:
Do you intend it?
CASSIO

Ha, ha, ha!

OTHELLO

Do you triumph, Roman? do you triumph?

CASSIO

I marry her! what? a customer! Prithee, bear some
charity to my wit: do not think it so unwholesome.
Ha, ha, ha!

OTHELLO

So, so, so, so: they laugh that win.

IAGO

'Faith, the cry goes that you shall marry her.

CASSIO

Prithee, say true.

IAGO

I am a very villain else.

OTHELLO

Have you scored me? Well.

CASSIO

This is the monkey's own giving out: she is
persuaded I will marry her, out of her own love and
flattery, not out of my promise.

OTHELLO

Iago beckons me; now he begins the story.

CASSIO

She was here even now; she haunts me in every place.
I was the other day talking on the sea-bank with
certain Venetians; and thither comes the bauble,
and, by this hand, she falls me thus about my neck--

OTHELLO

Crying 'O dear Cassio!' as it were: his gesture
imports it.

CASSIO

So hangs, and lolls, and weeps upon me; so hales,
and pulls me: ha, ha, ha!

OTHELLO

Now he tells how she plucked him to my chamber. O,
I see that nose of yours, but not that dog I shall
throw it to.

CASSIO

Well, I must leave her company.

IAGO

Before me! look, where she comes.

CASSIO

'Tis such another fitchew! marry a perfumed one.

Enter BIANCA

What do you mean by this haunting of me?

BIANCA

Let the devil and his dam haunt you! What did you
mean by that same handkerchief you gave me even
now?
I was a fine fool to take it. I must take out the
work?--A likely piece of work, that you should find
it in your chamber, and not know who left it there!
This is some minx's token, and I must take out the
work? There; give it your hobby-horse: wheresoever
you had it, I'll take out no work on't.

CASSIO

How now, my sweet Bianca! how now! how now!

OTHELLO

By heaven, that should be my handkerchief!

BIANCA

An you'll come to supper to-night, you may; an you
will not, come when you are next prepared for.

Exit

IAGO

After her, after her.

CASSIO

'Faith, I must; she'll rail in the street else.

IAGO

Will you sup there?

CASSIO

'Faith, I intend so.

IAGO

Well, I may chance to see you; for I would very fain speak with you.

CASSIO

Prithee, come; will you?

IAGO

Go to; say no more.

Exit CASSIO

OTHELLO

[Advancing] How shall I murder him, Iago?

IAGO

Did you perceive how he laughed at his vice?

OTHELLO

O Iago!

IAGO

And did you see the handkerchief?

OTHELLO

Was that mine?

IAGO

Yours by this hand: and to see how he prizes the foolish woman your wife! she gave it him, and he hath given it his whore.

OTHELLO

I would have him nine years a-killing.
A fine woman! a fair woman! a sweet woman!

IAGO

Nay, you must forget that.

OTHELLO

Ay, let her rot, and perish, and be damned to-night;
for she shall not live: no, my heart is turned to
stone; I strike it, and it hurts my hand. O, the
world hath not a sweeter creature: she might lie by
an emperor's side and command him tasks.

IAGO

Nay, that's not your way.

OTHELLO

Hang her! I do but say what she is: so delicate
with her needle: an admirable musician: O! she
will sing the savageness out of a bear: of so high
and plenteous wit and invention:--

IAGO

She's the worse for all this.

OTHELLO

O, a thousand thousand times: and then, of so
gentle a condition!

IAGO

Ay, too gentle.

OTHELLO

Nay, that's certain: but yet the pity of it, Iago!
O Iago, the pity of it, Iago!

IAGO

If you are so fond over her iniquity, give her
patent to offend; for, if it touch not you, it comes
near nobody.

OTHELLO

I will chop her into messes: cuckold me!

IAGO

O, 'tis foul in her.

OTHELLO

With mine officer!

IAGO

That's fouler.

OTHELLO

Get me some poison, Iago; this night: I'll not
expostulate with her, lest her body and beauty
unprovide my mind again: this night, Iago.

IAGO

Do it not with poison, strangle her in her bed, even
the bed she hath contaminated.

OTHELLO

Good, good: the justice of it pleases: very good.

IAGO

And for Cassio, let me be his undertaker: you
shall hear more by midnight.

OTHELLO

Excellent good.

A trumpet within

What trumpet is that same?

IAGO

Something from Venice, sure. 'Tis Lodovico
Come from the duke: and, see, your wife is with him.

Enter LODOVICO, DESDEMONA, and Attendants

LODOVICO

Save you, worthy general!

OTHELLO

With all my heart, sir.

LODOVICO

The duke and senators of Venice greet you.

Gives him a letter

OTHELLO

I kiss the instrument of their pleasures.

Opens the letter, and reads

DESDEMONA
And what's the news, good cousin Lodovico?
IAGO
I am very glad to see you, signior
Welcome to Cyprus.
LODOVICO
I thank you. How does Lieutenant Cassio?
IAGO
Lives, sir.
DESDEMONA
Cousin, there's fall'n between him and my lord
An unkind breach: but you shall make all well.
OTHELLO
Are you sure of that?
DESDEMONA
My lord?
OTHELLO
[Reads] 'This fail you not to do, as you will--'
LODOVICO
He did not call; he's busy in the paper.
Is there division 'twixt my lord and Cassio?
DESDEMONA
A most unhappy one: I would do much
To atone them, for the love I bear to Cassio.
OTHELLO
Fire and brimstone!
DESDEMONA
My lord?
OTHELLO
Are you wise?
DESDEMONA

What, is he angry?
LODOVICO
  May be the letter moved him;
  For, as I think, they do command him home,
  Deputing Cassio in his government.
DESDEMONA
  Trust me, I am glad on't.
OTHELLO
  Indeed!
DESDEMONA
  My lord?
OTHELLO
  I am glad to see you mad.
DESDEMONA
  Why, sweet Othello,--
OTHELLO
  [Striking her] Devil!
DESDEMONA
  I have not deserved this.
LODOVICO
  My lord, this would not be believed in Venice,
  Though I should swear I saw't: 'tis very much:
  Make her amends; she weeps.
OTHELLO
  O devil, devil!
  If that the earth could teem with woman's tears,
  Each drop she falls would prove a crocodile.
  Out of my sight!
DESDEMONA
  I will not stay to offend you.

                                        Going

LODOVICO
  Truly, an obedient lady:

I do beseech your lordship, call her back.
OTHELLO
  Mistress!
DESDEMONA
  My lord?
OTHELLO
  What would you with her, sir?
LODOVICO
  Who, I, my lord?
OTHELLO
  Ay; you did wish that I would make her turn:
  Sir, she can turn, and turn, and yet go on,
  And turn again; and she can weep, sir, weep;
  And she's obedient, as you say, obedient,
  Very obedient. Proceed you in your tears.
  Concerning this, sir,--O well-painted passion!--
  I am commanded home. Get you away;
  I'll send for you anon. Sir, I obey the mandate,
  And will return to Venice. Hence, avaunt!

                Exit DESDEMONA

  Cassio shall have my place. And, sir, tonight,
  I do entreat that we may sup together:
  You are welcome, sir, to Cyprus.--Goats and monkeys!

                Exit

LODOVICO
  Is this the noble Moor whom our full senate
  Call all in all sufficient? Is this the nature
  Whom passion could not shake? whose solid virtue
  The shot of accident, nor dart of chance,
  Could neither graze nor pierce?
IAGO

He is much changed.
LODOVICO
Are his wits safe? is he not light of brain?
IAGO
He's that he is: I may not breathe my censure
What he might be: if what he might he is not,
I would to heaven he were!
LODOVICO
What, strike his wife!
IAGO
'Faith, that was not so well; yet would I knew
That stroke would prove the worst!
LODOVICO
Is it his use?
Or did the letters work upon his blood,
And new-create this fault?
IAGO
Alas, alas!
It is not honesty in me to speak
What I have seen and known. You shall observe him,
And his own courses will denote him so
That I may save my speech: do but go after,
And mark how he continues.
LODOVICO
I am sorry that I am deceived in him.

Exeunt

SCENE II.

A room in the castle.

Enter OTHELLO and EMILIA

OTHELLO
You have seen nothing then?

EMILIA
Nor ever heard, nor ever did suspect.
OTHELLO
Yes, you have seen Cassio and she together.
EMILIA
But then I saw no harm, and then I heard
Each syllable that breath made up between them.
OTHELLO
What, did they never whisper?
EMILIA
Never, my lord.
OTHELLO
Nor send you out o' the way?
EMILIA
Never.
OTHELLO
To fetch her fan, her gloves, her mask, nor nothing?
EMILIA
Never, my lord.
OTHELLO
That's strange.
EMILIA
I durst, my lord, to wager she is honest,
Lay down my soul at stake: if you think other,
Remove your thought; it doth abuse your bosom.
If any wretch have put this in your head,
Let heaven requite it with the serpent's curse!
For, if she be not honest, chaste, and true,
There's no man happy; the purest of their wives
Is foul as slander.
OTHELLO
Bid her come hither: go.

Exit EMILIA

She says enough; yet she's a simple bawd
That cannot say as much. This is a subtle whore,
A closet lock and key of villanous secrets
And yet she'll kneel and pray; I have seen her do't.

Enter DESDEMONA with EMILIA

DESDEMONA
My lord, what is your will?
OTHELLO
Pray, chuck, come hither.
DESDEMONA
What is your pleasure?
OTHELLO
Let me see your eyes;
Look in my face.
DESDEMONA
What horrible fancy's this?
OTHELLO
[To EMILIA] Some of your function, mistress;
Leave procreants alone and shut the door;
Cough, or cry 'hem,' if any body come:
Your mystery, your mystery: nay, dispatch.

Exit EMILIA

DESDEMONA
Upon my knees, what doth your speech import?
I understand a fury in your words.
But not the words.
OTHELLO
Why, what art thou?
DESDEMONA
Your wife, my lord; your true
And loyal wife.

OTHELLO

Come, swear it, damn thyself
Lest, being like one of heaven, the devils themselves
Should fear to seize thee: therefore be double damn'd:
Swear thou art honest.

DESDEMONA

Heaven doth truly know it.

OTHELLO

Heaven truly knows that thou art false as hell.

DESDEMONA

To whom, my lord? with whom? how am I false?

OTHELLO

O Desdemona! away! away! away!

DESDEMONA

Alas the heavy day! Why do you weep?
Am I the motive of these tears, my lord?
If haply you my father do suspect
An instrument of this your calling back,
Lay not your blame on me: If you have lost him,
Why, I have lost him too.

OTHELLO

Had it pleased heaven
To try me with affliction; had they rain'd
All kinds of sores and shames on my bare head.
Steep'd me in poverty to the very lips,
Given to captivity me and my utmost hopes,
I should have found in some place of my soul
A drop of patience: but, alas, to make me
A fixed figure for the time of scorn
To point his slow unmoving finger at!
Yet could I bear that too; well, very well:
But there, where I have garner'd up my heart,
Where either I must live, or bear no life;
The fountain from the which my current runs,

Or else dries up; to be discarded thence!
Or keep it as a cistern for foul toads
To knot and gender in! Turn thy complexion there,
Patience, thou young and rose-lipp'd cherubin,--
Ay, there, look grim as hell!

DESDEMONA
I hope my noble lord esteems me honest.

OTHELLO
O, ay; as summer flies are in the shambles,
That quicken even with blowing. O thou weed,
Who art so lovely fair and smell'st so sweet
That the sense aches at thee, would thou hadst
ne'er been born!

DESDEMONA
Alas, what ignorant sin have I committed?

OTHELLO
Was this fair paper, this most goodly book,
Made to write 'whore' upon? What committed!
Committed! O thou public commoner!
I should make very forges of my cheeks,
That would to cinders burn up modesty,
Did I but speak thy deeds. What committed!
Heaven stops the nose at it and the moon winks,
The bawdy wind that kisses all it meets
Is hush'd within the hollow mine of earth,
And will not hear it. What committed!
Impudent strumpet!

DESDEMONA
By heaven, you do me wrong.

OTHELLO
Are you not a strumpet?

DESDEMONA
No, as I am a Christian:
If to preserve this vessel for my lord

From any other foul unlawful touch
Be not to be a strumpet, I am none.
OTHELLO
What, not a whore?
DESDEMONA
No, as I shall be saved.
OTHELLO
Is't possible?
DESDEMONA
O, heaven forgive us!
OTHELLO
I cry you mercy, then:
I took you for that cunning whore of Venice
That married with Othello.

Raising his voice

You, mistress,
That have the office opposite to Saint Peter,
And keep the gate of hell!

Re-enter EMILIA

You, you, ay, you!
We have done our course; there's money for your pains:
I pray you, turn the key and keep our counsel.

Exit

EMILIA
Alas, what does this gentleman conceive?
How do you, madam? how do you, my good lady?
DESDEMONA
'Faith, half asleep.
EMILIA
Good madam, what's the matter with my lord?

DESDEMONA
  With who?
EMILIA
  Why, with my lord, madam.
DESDEMONA
  Who is thy lord?
EMILIA
  He that is yours, sweet lady.
DESDEMONA
  I have none: do not talk to me, Emilia;
  I cannot weep; nor answer have I none,
  But what should go by water. Prithee, tonight
  Lay on my bed my wedding sheets: remember;
  And call thy husband hither.
EMILIA
  Here's a change indeed!

                              Exit

DESDEMONA
  'Tis meet I should be used so, very meet.
  How have I been behaved, that he might stick
  The small'st opinion on my least misuse?

            Re-enter EMILIA with IAGO

IAGO
  What is your pleasure, madam?
  How is't with you?
DESDEMONA
  I cannot tell. Those that do teach young babes
  Do it with gentle means and easy tasks:
  He might have chid me so; for, in good faith,
  I am a child to chiding.
IAGO

What's the matter, lady?

EMILIA

Alas, Iago, my lord hath so bewhored her.
Thrown such despite and heavy terms upon her,
As true hearts cannot bear.

DESDEMONA

Am I that name, Iago?

IAGO

What name, fair lady?

DESDEMONA

Such as she says my lord did say I was.

EMILIA

He call'd her whore: a beggar in his drink
Could not have laid such terms upon his callat.

IAGO

Why did he so?

DESDEMONA

I do not know; I am sure I am none such.

IAGO

Do not weep, do not weep. Alas the day!

EMILIA

Hath she forsook so many noble matches,
Her father and her country and her friends,
To be call'd whore? would it not make one weep?

DESDEMONA

It is my wretched fortune.

IAGO

Beshrew him for't!
How comes this trick upon him?

DESDEMONA

Nay, heaven doth know.

EMILIA

I will be hang'd, if some eternal villain,
Some busy and insinuating rogue,

Some cogging, cozening slave, to get some office,
Have not devised this slander; I'll be hang'd else.

IAGO

Fie, there is no such man; it is impossible.

DESDEMONA

If any such there be, heaven pardon him!

EMILIA

A halter pardon him! and hell gnaw his bones!
Why should he call her whore? who keeps her
company?
What place? what time? what form? what likelihood?
The Moor's abused by some most villanous knave,
Some base notorious knave, some scurvy fellow.
O heaven, that such companions thou'ldst unfold,
And put in every honest hand a whip
To lash the rascals naked through the world
Even from the east to the west!

IAGO

Speak within door.

EMILIA

O, fie upon them! Some such squire he was
That turn'd your wit the seamy side without,
And made you to suspect me with the Moor.

IAGO

You are a fool; go to.

DESDEMONA

O good Iago,
What shall I do to win my lord again?
Good friend, go to him; for, by this light of heaven,
I know not how I lost him. Here I kneel:
If e'er my will did trespass 'gainst his love,
Either in discourse of thought or actual deed,
Or that mine eyes, mine ears, or any sense,
Delighted them in any other form;

Or that I do not yet, and ever did.
And ever will--though he do shake me off
To beggarly divorcement--love him dearly,
Comfort forswear me! Unkindness may do much;
And his unkindness may defeat my life,
But never taint my love. I cannot say 'whore:'
It does abhor me now I speak the word;
To do the act that might the addition earn
Not the world's mass of vanity could make me.

IAGO

I pray you, be content; 'tis but his humour:
The business of the state does him offence,
And he does chide with you.

DESDEMONA

If 'twere no other--

IAGO

'Tis but so, I warrant.

Trumpets within

Hark, how these instruments summon to supper!
The messengers of Venice stay the meat;
Go in, and weep not; all things shall be well.

Exeunt DESDEMONA and EMILIA

Enter RODERIGO

How now, Roderigo!

RODERIGO

I do not find that thou dealest justly with me.

IAGO

What in the contrary?

RODERIGO

Every day thou daffest me with some device, Iago;

and rather, as it seems to me now, keepest from me
all conveniency than suppliest me with the least
advantage of hope. I will indeed no longer endure
it, nor am I yet persuaded to put up in peace what
already I have foolishly suffered.

IAGO

Will you hear me, Roderigo?

RODERIGO

'Faith, I have heard too much, for your words and
performances are no kin together.

IAGO

You charge me most unjustly.

RODERIGO

With nought but truth. I have wasted myself out of
my means. The jewels you have had from me to
deliver to Desdemona would half have corrupted a
votarist: you have told me she hath received them
and returned me expectations and comforts of sudden
respect and acquaintance, but I find none.

IAGO

Well; go to; very well.

RODERIGO

Very well! go to! I cannot go to, man; nor 'tis
not very well: nay, I think it is scurvy, and begin
to find myself fobbed in it.

IAGO

Very well.

RODERIGO

I tell you 'tis not very well. I will make myself
known to Desdemona: if she will return me my
jewels, I will give over my suit and repent my
unlawful solicitation; if not, assure yourself I
will seek satisfaction of you.

IAGO

You have said now.

RODERIGO

Ay, and said nothing but what I protest intendment of
doing.

IAGO

Why, now I see there's mettle in thee, and even from
this instant to build on thee a better opinion than
ever before. Give me thy hand, Roderigo: thou hast
taken against me a most just exception; but yet, I
protest, I have dealt most directly in thy affair.

RODERIGO

It hath not appeared.

IAGO

I grant indeed it hath not appeared, and your
suspicion is not without wit and judgment. But,
Roderigo, if thou hast that in thee indeed, which I
have greater reason to believe now than ever, I mean
purpose, courage and valour, this night show it: if
thou the next night following enjoy not Desdemona,
take me from this world with treachery and devise
engines for my life.

RODERIGO

Well, what is it? is it within reason and compass?

IAGO

Sir, there is especial commission come from Venice
to depute Cassio in Othello's place.

RODERIGO

Is that true? why, then Othello and Desdemona
return again to Venice.

IAGO

O, no; he goes into Mauritania and takes away with
him the fair Desdemona, unless his abode be
lingered here by some accident: wherein none can be
so determinate as the removing of Cassio.

RODERIGO
How do you mean, removing of him?
IAGO
Why, by making him uncapable of Othello's place;
knocking out his brains.
RODERIGO
And that you would have me to do?
IAGO
Ay, if you dare do yourself a profit and a right.
He sups to-night with a harlotry, and thither will I
go to him: he knows not yet of his horrorable
fortune. If you will watch his going thence, which
I will fashion to fall out between twelve and one,
you may take him at your pleasure: I will be near
to second your attempt, and he shall fall between
us. Come, stand not amazed at it, but go along with
me; I will show you such a necessity in his death
that you shall think yourself bound to put it on
him. It is now high suppertime, and the night grows
to waste: about it.
RODERIGO
I will hear further reason for this.
IAGO
And you shall be satisfied.

Exeunt

SCENE III.

Another room In the castle.

*Enter OTHELLO, LODOVICO, DESDEMONA, EMILIA and
Attendants*

LODOVICO
I do beseech you, sir, trouble yourself no further.

OTHELLO
  O, pardon me: 'twill do me good to walk.
LODOVICO
  Madam, good night; I humbly thank your ladyship.
DESDEMONA
  Your honour is most welcome.
OTHELLO
  Will you walk, sir?
  O,--Desdemona,--
DESDEMONA
  My lord?
OTHELLO
  Get you to bed on the instant; I will be returned
  forthwith: dismiss your attendant there: look it be done.
DESDEMONA
  I will, my lord.

  Exeunt OTHELLO, LODOVICO, and Attendants

EMILIA
  How goes it now? he looks gentler than he did.
DESDEMONA
  He says he will return incontinent:
  He hath commanded me to go to bed,
  And bade me to dismiss you.
EMILIA
  Dismiss me!
DESDEMONA
  It was his bidding: therefore, good Emilia,.
  Give me my nightly wearing, and adieu:
  We must not now displease him.
EMILIA
  I would you had never seen him!
DESDEMONA
  So would not I..   my love doth so approve him,

That even his stubbornness, his cheques, his frowns--
Prithee, unpin me,--have grace and favour in them.
EMILIA
I have laid those sheets you bade me on the bed.
DESDEMONA
All's one. Good faith, how foolish are our minds!
If I do die before thee prithee, shroud me
In one of those same sheets.
EMILIA
Come, come you talk.
DESDEMONA
My mother had a maid call'd Barbara:
She was in love, and he she loved proved mad
And did forsake her: she had a song of 'willow;'
An old thing 'twas, but it express'd her fortune,
And she died singing it: that song to-night
Will not go from my mind; I have much to do,
But to go hang my head all at one side,
And sing it like poor Barbara. Prithee, dispatch.
EMILIA
Shall I go fetch your night-gown?
DESDEMONA
No, unpin me here.
This Lodovico is a proper man.
EMILIA
A very handsome man.
DESDEMONA
He speaks well.
EMILIA
I know a lady in Venice would have walked barefoot
to Palestine for a touch of his nether lip.
DESDEMONA
[Singing] The poor soul sat sighing by a sycamore tree,
Sing all a green willow:

Her hand on her bosom, her head on her knee,
Sing willow, willow, willow:
The fresh streams ran by her, and murmur'd her moans;
Sing willow, willow, willow;
Her salt tears fell from her, and soften'd the stones;
Lay by these:--

Singing

Sing willow, willow, willow;
Prithee, hie thee; he'll come anon:--

Singing

Sing all a green willow must be my garland.
Let nobody blame him; his scorn I approve,-
Nay, that's not next.--Hark! who is't that knocks?
EMILIA
It's the wind.
DESDEMONA
[Singing] I call'd my love false love; but what
said he then?
Sing willow, willow, willow:
If I court moe women, you'll couch with moe men!
So, get thee gone; good night Ate eyes do itch;
Doth that bode weeping?
EMILIA
'Tis neither here nor there.
DESDEMONA
I have heard it said so. O, these men, these men!
Dost thou in conscience think,--tell me, Emilia,--
That there be women do abuse their husbands
In such gross kind?
EMILIA
There be some such, no question.

DESDEMONA

Wouldst thou do such a deed for all the world?

EMILIA

Why, would not you?

DESDEMONA

No, by this heavenly light!

EMILIA

Nor I neither by this heavenly light;
I might do't as well i' the dark.

DESDEMONA

Wouldst thou do such a deed for all the world?

EMILIA

The world's a huge thing: it is a great price.
For a small vice.

DESDEMONA

In troth, I think thou wouldst not.

EMILIA

In troth, I think I should; and undo't when I had
done. Marry, I would not do such a thing for a
joint-ring, nor for measures of lawn, nor for
gowns, petticoats, nor caps, nor any petty
exhibition; but for the whole world,--why, who would
not make her husband a cuckold to make him a
monarch? I should venture purgatory for't.

DESDEMONA

Beshrew me, if I would do such a wrong
For the whole world.

EMILIA

Why the wrong is but a wrong i' the world: and
having the world for your labour, tis a wrong in your
own world, and you might quickly make it right.

DESDEMONA

I do not think there is any such woman.

EMILIA

Yes, a dozen; and as many to the vantage as would
store the world they played for.
But I do think it is their husbands' faults
If wives do fall: say that they slack their duties,
And pour our treasures into foreign laps,
Or else break out in peevish jealousies,
Throwing restraint upon us; or say they strike us,
Or scant our former having in despite;
Why, we have galls, and though we have some grace,
Yet have we some revenge. Let husbands know
Their wives have sense like them: they see and smell
And have their palates both for sweet and sour,
As husbands have. What is it that they do
When they change us for others? Is it sport?
I think it is: and doth affection breed it?
I think it doth: is't frailty that thus errs?
It is so too: and have not we affections,
Desires for sport, and frailty, as men have?
Then let them use us well: else let them know,
The ills we do, their ills instruct us so.

DESDEMONA

Good night, good night: heaven me such uses send,
Not to pick bad from bad, but by bad mend!

Exeunt

133

ACT V

SCENE I.

Cyprus. A street.

Enter IAGO and RODERIGO

IAGO

> Here, stand behind this bulk; straight will he come:
> Wear thy good rapier bare, and put it home:
> Quick, quick; fear nothing; I'll be at thy elbow:
> It makes us, or it mars us; think on that,
> And fix most firm thy resolution.

RODERIGO

> Be near at hand; I may miscarry in't.

IAGO

> Here, at thy hand: be bold, and take thy stand.

Retires

RODERIGO

> I have no great devotion to the deed;
> And yet he hath given me satisfying reasons:
> 'Tis but a man gone. Forth, my sword: he dies.

IAGO

> I have rubb'd this young quat almost to the sense,
> And he grows angry. Now, whether he kill Cassio,
> Or Cassio him, or each do kill the other,
> Every way makes my gain: live Roderigo,
> He calls me to a restitution large
> Of gold and jewels that I bobb'd from him,
> As gifts to Desdemona;
> It must not be: if Cassio do remain,
> He hath a daily beauty in his life

That makes me ugly; and, besides, the Moor
May unfold me to him; there stand I in much peril:
No, he must die. But so: I hear him coming.

Enter CASSIO

RODERIGO
I know his gait, 'tis he.--Villain, thou diest!

Makes a pass at CASSIO

CASSIO
That thrust had been mine enemy indeed,
But that my coat is better than thou know'st
I will make proof of thine.

Draws, and wounds RODERIGO

RODERIGO
O, I am slain!

IAGO from behind wounds CASSIO in the leg, and exit

CASSIO
I am maim'd for ever. Help, ho! murder! murder!

Falls

Enter OTHELLO

OTHELLO
The voice of Cassio: Iago keeps his word.
RODERIGO
O, villain that I am!
OTHELLO
It is even so.
CASSIO

O, help, ho! light! a surgeon!

OTHELLO

'Tis he:--O brave Iago, honest and just,
That hast such noble sense of thy friend's wrong!
Thou teachest me. Minion, your dear lies dead,
And your unblest fate hies: strumpet, I come.
Forth of my heart those charms, thine eyes, are blotted;
Thy bed, lust-stain'd, shall with lust's blood be spotted.

Exit

Enter LODOVICO and GRATIANO

CASSIO

What, ho! no watch? no passage? murder! murder!

GRATIANO

'Tis some mischance; the cry is very direful.

CASSIO

O, help!

LODOVICO

Hark!

RODERIGO

O wretched villain!

LODOVICO

Two or three groan: it is a heavy night:
These may be counterfeits: let's think't unsafe
To come in to the cry without more help.

RODERIGO

Nobody come? then shall I bleed to death.

LODOVICO

Hark!

Re-enter IAGO, with a light

GRATIANO

Here's one comes in his shirt, with light and weapons.

IAGO

Who's there? whose noise is this that ones on murder?

LODOVICO

We do not know.

IAGO

Did not you hear a cry?

CASSIO

Here, here! for heaven's sake, help me!

IAGO

What's the matter?

GRATIANO

This is Othello's ancient, as I take it.

LODOVICO

The same indeed; a very valiant fellow.

IAGO

What are you here that cry so grievously?

CASSIO

Iago? O, I am spoil'd, undone by villains!

Give me some help.

IAGO

O me, lieutenant! what villains have done this?

CASSIO

I think that one of them is hereabout,

And cannot make away.

IAGO

O treacherous villains!

What are you there? come in, and give some help.

To LODOVICO and GRATIANO

RODERIGO

O, help me here!

CASSIO

That's one of them.

IAGO

O murderous slave! O villain!

Stabs RODERIGO

RODERIGO

O damn'd Iago! O inhuman dog!

IAGO

Kill men i' the dark!--Where be these bloody thieves?--
How silent is this town!--Ho! murder! murder!--
What may you be? are you of good or evil?

LODOVICO

As you shall prove us, praise us.

IAGO

Signior Lodovico?

LODOVICO

He, sir.

IAGO

I cry you mercy. Here's Cassio hurt by villains.

GRATIANO

Cassio!

IAGO

How is't, brother!

CASSIO

My leg is cut in two.

IAGO

Marry, heaven forbid!
Light, gentlemen; I'll bind it with my shirt.

Enter BIANCA

BIANCA

What is the matter, ho? who is't that cried?

IAGO

Who is't that cried!

BIANCA

O my dear Cassio! my sweet Cassio! O Cassio,
Cassio, Cassio!

IAGO

O notable strumpet! Cassio, may you suspect
Who they should be that have thus many led you?

CASSIO

No.

GRATIANO

I am to find you thus: I have been to seek you.

IAGO

Lend me a garter. So. O, for a chair,
To bear him easily hence!

BIANCA

Alas, he faints! O Cassio, Cassio, Cassio!

IAGO

Gentlemen all, I do suspect this trash
To be a party in this injury.
Patience awhile, good Cassio. Come, come;
Lend me a light. Know we this face or no?
Alas my friend and my dear countryman
Roderigo! no:--yes, sure: O heaven! Roderigo.

GRATIANO

What, of Venice?

IAGO

Even he, sir; did you know him?

GRATIANO

Know him! ay.

IAGO

Signior Gratiano? I cry you gentle pardon;
These bloody accidents must excuse my manners,
That so neglected you.

GRATIANO

I am glad to see you.

IAGO
How do you, Cassio? O, a chair, a chair!
GRATIANO
Roderigo!
IAGO
He, he 'tis he.

A chair brought in

O, that's well said; the chair!
GRATIANO
Some good man bear him carefully from hence;
I'll fetch the general's surgeon.

To BIANCA

For you, mistress,
Save you your labour. He that lies slain
here, Cassio,
Was my dear friend: what malice was between you?
CASSIO
None in the world; nor do I know the man.
IAGO
[To BIANCA] What, look you pale? O, bear him out
o' the air.

CASSIO and RODERIGO are borne off

Stay you, good gentlemen. Look you pale, mistress?
Do you perceive the gastness of her eye?
Nay, if you stare, we shall hear more anon.
Behold her well; I pray you, look upon her:
Do you see, gentlemen? nay, guiltiness will speak,
Though tongues were out of use.

Enter EMILIA

EMILIA

'Las, what's the matter? what's the matter, husband?

IAGO

Cassio hath here been set on in the dark
By Roderigo and fellows that are scaped:
He's almost slain, and Roderigo dead.

EMILIA

Alas, good gentleman! alas, good Cassio!

IAGO

This is the fruit of whoring. Prithee, Emilia,
Go know of Cassio where he supp'd to-night.

To BIANCA

What, do you shake at that?

BIANCA

He supp'd at my house; but I therefore shake not.

IAGO

O, did he so? I charge you, go with me.

EMILIA

Fie, fie upon thee, strumpet!

BIANCA

I am no strumpet; but of life as honest
As you that thus abuse me.

EMILIA

As I! foh! fie upon thee!

IAGO

Kind gentlemen, let's go see poor Cassio dress'd.
Come, mistress, you must tell's another tale.
Emilia run you to the citadel,
And tell my lord and lady what hath happ'd.
Will you go on? I pray.

Aside

This is the night
That either makes me or fordoes me quite.

Exeunt

SCENE II.

A bedchamber in the castle: DESDEMONA in bed asleep;

a light burning.

Enter OTHELLO

OTHELLO
It is the cause, it is the cause, my soul,--
Let me not name it to you, you chaste stars!--
It is the cause. Yet I'll not shed her blood;
Nor scar that whiter skin of hers than snow,
And smooth as monumental alabaster.
Yet she must die, else she'll betray more men.
Put out the light, and then put out the light:
If I quench thee, thou flaming minister,
I can again thy former light restore,
Should I repent me: but once put out thy light,
Thou cunning'st pattern of excelling nature,
I know not where is that Promethean heat
That can thy light relume. When I have pluck'd the rose,
I cannot give it vital growth again.
It must needs wither: I'll smell it on the tree.

Kissing her

Ah balmy breath, that dost almost persuade
Justice to break her sword! One more, one more.
Be thus when thou art dead, and I will kill thee,
And love thee after. One more, and this the last:

So sweet was ne'er so fatal. I must weep,
But they are cruel tears: this sorrow's heavenly;
It strikes where it doth love. She wakes.

DESDEMONA

Who's there? Othello?

OTHELLO

Ay. Desdemona.

DESDEMONA

Will you come to bed, my lord?

OTHELLO

Have you pray'd to-night, Desdemona?

DESDEMONA

Ay, my lord.

OTHELLO

If you bethink yourself of any crime
Unreconciled as yet to heaven and grace,
Solicit for it straight.

DESDEMONA

Alas, my lord, what do you mean by that?

OTHELLO

Well, do it, and be brief; I will walk by:
I would not kill thy unprepared spirit;
No; heaven forfend! I would not kill thy soul.

DESDEMONA

Talk you of killing?

OTHELLO

Ay, I do.

DESDEMONA

Then heaven
Have mercy on me!

OTHELLO

Amen, with all my heart!

DESDEMONA

If you say so, I hope you will not kill me.

OTHELLO
  Hum!
DESDEMONA
  And yet I fear you; for you are fatal then
  When your eyes roll so: why I should fear I know not,
  Since guiltiness I know not; but yet I feel I fear.
OTHELLO
  Think on thy sins.
DESDEMONA
  They are loves I bear to you.
OTHELLO
  Ay, and for that thou diest.
DESDEMONA
  That death's unnatural that kills for loving.
  Alas, why gnaw you so your nether lip?
  Some bloody passion shakes your very frame:
  These are portents; but yet I hope, I hope,
  They do not point on me.
OTHELLO
  Peace, and be still!
DESDEMONA
  I will so. What's the matter?
OTHELLO
  That handkerchief which I so loved and gave thee
  Thou gavest to Cassio.
DESDEMONA
  No, by my life and soul!
  Send for the man, and ask him.
OTHELLO
  Sweet soul, take heed,
  Take heed of perjury; thou art on thy deathbed.
DESDEMONA
  Ay, but not yet to die.
OTHELLO

Yes, presently:
Therefore confess thee freely of thy sin;
For to deny each article with oath
Cannot remove nor choke the strong conception
That I do groan withal. Thou art to die.
DESDEMONA
Then Lord have mercy on me!
OTHELLO
I say, amen.
DESDEMONA
And have you mercy too! I never did
Offend you in my life; never loved Cassio
But with such general warranty of heaven
As I might love: I never gave him token.
OTHELLO
By heaven, I saw my handkerchief in's hand.
O perjured woman! thou dost stone my heart,
And makest me call what I intend to do
A murder, which I thought a sacrifice:
I saw the handkerchief.
DESDEMONA
He found it then;
I never gave it him: send for him hither;
Let him confess a truth.
OTHELLO
He hath confess'd.
DESDEMONA
What, my lord?
OTHELLO
That he hath used thee.
DESDEMONA
How? unlawfully?
OTHELLO
Ay.

DESDEMONA
He will not say so.
OTHELLO
No, his mouth is stopp'd;
Honest Iago hath ta'en order for't.
DESDEMONA
O! my fear interprets: what, is he dead?
OTHELLO
Had all his hairs been lives, my great revenge
Had stomach for them all.
DESDEMONA
Alas! he is betray'd and I undone.
OTHELLO
Out, strumpet! weep'st thou for him to my face?
DESDEMONA
O, banish me, my lord, but kill me not!
OTHELLO
Down, strumpet!
DESDEMONA
Kill me to-morrow: let me live to-night!
OTHELLO
Nay, if you strive--
DESDEMONA
But half an hour!
OTHELLO
Being done, there is no pause.
DESDEMONA
But while I say one prayer!
OTHELLO
It is too late.

He stifles her

EMILIA
[Within] My lord , my lord! what, ho! my lord, my lord!

146

OTHELLO
　What noise is this? Not dead? not yet quite dead?
　I that am cruel am yet merciful;
　I would not have thee linger in thy pain: So, so.
EMILIA
　[Within] What, ho! my lord, my lord!
OTHELLO
　Who's there?
EMILIA
　[Within] O, good my lord, I would speak a word with
　you!
OTHELLO
　Yes: 'tis Emilia. By and by. She's dead.
　'Tis like she comes to speak of Cassio's death.--
　The noise was here. Ha! no more moving?
　Still as the grave. Shall she come in? were't good?--
　I think she stirs again:--no. What's best to do?
　If she come in, she'll sure speak to my wife:
　My wife! my wife! what wife? I have no wife.
　O insupportable! O heavy hour!
　Methinks it should be now a huge eclipse
　Of sun and moon, and that the affrighted globe
　Should yawn at alteration.
EMILIA
　[Within] I do beseech you
　That I may speak with you, O, good my lord!
OTHELLO
　I had forgot thee: O, come in, Emilia;
　Soft; by and by. Let me the curtains draw.
　Where art thou?

Unlocks the door

Enter EMILIA

What's the matter with thee now?

EMILIA

O, my good lord, yonder's foul murders done!

OTHELLO

What, now?

EMILIA

But now, my lord.

OTHELLO

It is the very error of the moon;
She comes more nearer earth than she was wont,
And makes men mad.

EMILIA

Cassio, my lord, hath kill'd a young Venetian
Call'd Roderigo.

OTHELLO

Roderigo kill'd!
And Cassio kill'd!

EMILIA

No, Cassio is not kill'd.

OTHELLO

Not Cassio kill'd! then murder's out of tune,
And sweet revenge grows harsh.

DESDEMONA

O, falsely, falsely murder'd!

EMILIA

Alas, what cry is that?

OTHELLO

That! what?

EMILIA

Out, and alas! that was my lady's voice.
Help! help, ho! help! O lady, speak again!
Sweet Desdemona! O sweet mistress, speak!

DESDEMONA

A guiltless death I die.

EMILIA

O, who hath done this deed?

DESDEMONA

Nobody; I myself. Farewell

Commend me to my kind lord: O, farewell!

Dies

OTHELLO

Why, how should she be murder'd?

EMILIA

Alas, who knows?

OTHELLO

You heard her say herself, it was not I.

EMILIA

She said so: I must needs report the truth.

OTHELLO

She's, like a liar, gone to burning hell:

'Twas I that kill'd her.

EMILIA

O, the more angel she,

And you the blacker devil!

OTHELLO

She turn'd to folly, and she was a whore.

EMILIA

Thou dost belie her, and thou art a devil.

OTHELLO

She was false as water.

EMILIA

Thou art rash as fire, to say

That she was false: O, she was heavenly true!

OTHELLO

Cassio did top her; ask thy husband else.

O, I were damn'd beneath all depth in hell,

But that I did proceed upon just grounds
To this extremity. Thy husband knew it all.
EMILIA
My husband!
OTHELLO
Thy husband.
EMILIA
That she was false to wedlock?
OTHELLO
Ay, with Cassio. Nay, had she been true,
If heaven would make me such another world
Of one entire and Perfect chrysolite,
I'ld not have sold her for it.
EMILIA
My husband!
OTHELLO
Ay, 'twas he that told me first:
An honest man he is, and hates the slime
That sticks on filthy deeds.
EMILIA
My husband!
OTHELLO
What needs this iteration, woman? I say thy husband.
EMILIA
O mistress, villany hath made mocks with love,
My husband say that she was false!
OTHELLO
He, woman;
I say thy husband: dost understand the word?
My friend, thy husband, honest, honest Iago.
EMILIA
If he say so, may his pernicious soul
Rot half a grain a day! he lies to the heart:
She was too fond of her most filthy bargain.

OTHELLO

Ha!

EMILIA

Do thy worst:

This deed of thine is no more worthy heaven

Than thou wast worthy her.

OTHELLO

Peace, you were best.

EMILIA

Thou hast not half that power to do me harm

As I have to be hurt. O gull! O dolt!

As ignorant as dirt! thou hast done a deed--

I care not for thy sword; I'll make thee known,

Though I lost twenty lives.--Help! help, ho! help!

The Moor hath kill'd my mistress! Murder! murder!

Enter MONTANO, GRATIANO, IAGO, and others

MONTANO

What is the matter? How now, general!

EMILIA

O, are you come, Iago? you have done well,

That men must lay their murders on your neck.

GRATIANO

What is the matter?

EMILIA

Disprove this villain, if thou be'st a man:

He says thou told'st him that his wife was false:

I know thou didst not, thou'rt not such a villain:

Speak, for my heart is full.

IAGO

I told him what I thought, and told no more

Than what he found himself was apt and true.

EMILIA

But did you ever tell him she was false?

151

IAGO

I did.

EMILIA

You told a lie, an odious, damned lie;

Upon my soul, a lie, a wicked lie.

She false with Cassio!--did you say with Cassio?

IAGO

With Cassio, mistress. Go to, charm your tongue.

EMILIA

I will not charm my tongue; I am bound to speak:

My mistress here lies murder'd in her bed,--

All

O heavens forfend!

EMILIA

And your reports have set the murder on.

OTHELLO

Nay, stare not, masters: it is true, indeed.

GRATIANO

'Tis a strange truth.

MONTANO

O monstrous act!

EMILIA

Villany, villany, villany!

I think upon't, I think: I smell't: O villany!--

I thought so then:--I'll kill myself for grief:--

O villany, villany!

IAGO

What, are you mad? I charge you, get you home.

EMILIA

Good gentlemen, let me have leave to speak:

'Tis proper I obey him, but not now.

Perchance, Iago, I will ne'er go home.

OTHELLO

O! O! O!

He falls on the bed

EMILIA

    Nay, lay thee down and roar;

    For thou hast kill'd the sweetest innocent

    That e'er did lift up eye.

OTHELLO

    [Rising] O, she was foul!

    I scarce did know you, uncle: there lies your niece,

    Whose breath, indeed, these hands have newly stopp'd:

    I know this act shows horrible and grim.

GRATIANO

    Poor Desdemona! I am glad thy father's dead:

    Thy match was mortal to him, and pure grief

    Shore his old thread in twain: did he live now,

    This sight would make him do a desperate turn,

    Yea, curse his better angel from his side,

    And fall to reprobation.

OTHELLO

    'Tis pitiful; but yet Iago knows

    That she with Cassio hath the act of shame

    A thousand times committed; Cassio confess'd it:

    And she did gratify his amorous works

    With that recognizance and pledge of love

    Which I first gave her; I saw it in his hand:

    It was a handkerchief, an antique token

    My father gave my mother.

EMILIA

    O heaven! O heavenly powers!

IAGO

    Come, hold your peace.

EMILIA

    'Twill out, 'twill out: I peace!

    No, I will speak as liberal as the north:

Let heaven and men and devils, let them all,
All, all, cry shame against me, yet I'll speak.
IAGO
Be wise, and get you home.
EMILIA
I will not.

IAGO offers to stab EMILIA

GRATIANO
Fie!
Your sword upon a woman?
EMILIA
O thou dull Moor! that handkerchief thou speak'st of
I found by fortune and did give my husband;
For often, with a solemn earnestness,
More than indeed belong'd to such a trifle,
He begg'd of me to steal it.
IAGO
Villanous whore!
EMILIA
She give it Cassio! no, alas! I found it,
And I did give't my husband.
IAGO
Filth, thou liest!
EMILIA
By heaven, I do not, I do not, gentlemen.
O murderous coxcomb! what should such a fool
Do with so good a woman?
OTHELLO
Are there no stones in heaven
But what serve for the thunder?--Precious villain!

*He runs at IAGO IAGO, from behind, stabs EMILIA, and
exit*

GRATIANO
    The woman falls; sure, he hath kill'd his wife.
EMILIA
    Ay, ay: O, lay me by my mistress' side.
GRATIANO
    He's gone, but his wife's kill'd.
MONTANO
    'Tis a notorious villain. Take you this weapon,
    Which I have here recover'd from the Moor:
    Come, guard the door without; let him not pass,
    But kill him rather. I'll after that same villain,
    For 'tis a damned slave.

Exeunt MONTANO and GRATIANO

OTHELLO
    I am not valiant neither,
    But ever puny whipster gets my sword:
    But why should honour outlive honesty?
    Let it go all.
EMILIA
    What did thy song bode, lady?
    Hark, canst thou hear me? I will play the swan.
    And die in music.

Singing

Willow, willow, willow,--
Moor, she was chaste; she loved thee, cruel Moor;
So come my soul to bliss, as I speak true;
So speaking as I think, I die, I die.

Dies

OTHELLO

I have another weapon in this chamber;
It is a sword of Spain, the ice-brook's temper:--
O, here it is. Uncle, I must come forth.
GRATIANO
[Within] If thou attempt it, it will cost thee dear:
Thou hast no weapon, and perforce must suffer.
OTHELLO
Look in upon me then and speak with me,
Or, naked as I am, I will assault thee.

Re-enter GRATIANO

GRATIANO
What is the matter?
OTHELLO
Behold, I have a weapon;
A better never did itself sustain
Upon a soldier's thigh: I have seen the day,
That, with this little arm and this good sword,
I have made my way through more impediments
Than twenty times your stop: but, O vain boast!
Who can control his fate? 'tis not so now.
Be not afraid, though you do see me weapon'd;
Here is my journey's end, here is my butt,
And very sea-mark of my utmost sail.
Do you go back dismay'd? 'tis a lost fear;
Man but a rush against Othello's breast,
And he retires. Where should Othello go?
Now, how dost thou look now? O ill-starr'd wench!
Pale as thy smock! when we shall meet at compt,
This look of thine will hurl my soul from heaven,
And fiends will snatch at it. Cold, cold, my girl!
Even like thy chastity. O cursed slave!
Whip me, ye devils,
From the possession of this heavenly sight!

Blow me about in winds! roast me in sulphur!
Wash me in steep-down gulfs of liquid fire!
O Desdemona! Desdemona! dead!
Oh! Oh! Oh!

Enter LODOVICO. MONTANO, CASSIO carried in a chair,
and Officers with IAGO, prisoner

LODOVICO
Where is this rash and most unfortunate man?
OTHELLO
That's he that was Othello: here I am.
LODOVICO
Where is that viper? bring the villain forth.
OTHELLO
I look down towards his feet; but that's a fable.
If that thou best a devil, I cannot kill thee.

Wounds IAGO

LODOVICO
Wrench his sword from him.
IAGO
I bleed, sir; but not kill'd.
OTHELLO
I am not sorry neither: I'ld have thee live;
For, in my sense, 'tis happiness to die.
LODOVICO
O thou Othello, thou wert once so good,
Fall'n in the practise of a damned slave,
What shall be said to thee?
OTHELLO
Why, any thing:
An honourable murderer, if you will;
For nought I did in hate, but all in honour.

LODOVICO

This wretch hath part confess'd his villany:
Did you and he consent in Cassio's death?

OTHELLO

Ay.

CASSIO

Dear general, I never gave you cause.

OTHELLO

I do believe it, and I ask your pardon.
Will you, I pray, demand that demi-devil
Why he hath thus ensnared my soul and body?

IAGO

Demand me nothing: what you know, you know:
From this time forth I never will speak word.

LODOVICO

What, not to pray?

GRATIANO

Torments will ope your lips.

OTHELLO

Well, thou dost best.

LODOVICO

Sir, you shall understand what hath befall'n,
Which, as I think, you know not. Here is a letter
Found in the pocket of the slain Roderigo;
And here another: the one of them imports
The death of Cassio to be undertook
By Roderigo.

OTHELLO

O villain!

CASSIO

Most heathenish and most gross!

LODOVICO

Now here's another discontented paper,
Found in his pocket too; and this, it seems,

Roderigo meant to have sent this damned villain;
But that belike Iago in the interim
Came in and satisfied him.

OTHELLO

O the pernicious caitiff!
How came you, Cassio, by that handkerchief
That was my wife's?

CASSIO

I found it in my chamber:
And he himself confess'd but even now
That there he dropp'd it for a special purpose
Which wrought to his desire.

OTHELLO

O fool! fool! fool!

CASSIO

There is besides in Roderigo's letter,
How he upbraids Iago, that he made him
Brave me upon the watch; whereon it came
That I was cast: and even but now he spake,
After long seeming dead, Iago hurt him,
Iago set him on.

LODOVICO

You must forsake this room, and go with us:
Your power and your command is taken off,
And Cassio rules in Cyprus. For this slave,
If there be any cunning cruelty
That can torment him much and hold him long,
It shall be his. You shall close prisoner rest,
Till that the nature of your fault be known
To the Venetian state. Come, bring him away.

OTHELLO

Soft you; a word or two before you go.
I have done the state some service, and they know't.
No more of that. I pray you, in your letters,

When you shall these unlucky deeds relate,
Speak of me as I am; nothing extenuate,
Nor set down aught in malice: then must you speak
Of one that loved not wisely but too well;
Of one not easily jealous, but being wrought
Perplex'd in the extreme; of one whose hand,
Like the base Indian, threw a pearl away
Richer than all his tribe; of one whose subdued eyes,
Albeit unused to the melting mood,
Drop tears as fast as the Arabian trees
Their medicinal gum. Set you down this;
And say besides, that in Aleppo once,
Where a malignant and a turban'd Turk
Beat a Venetian and traduced the state,
I took by the throat the circumcised dog,
And smote him, thus.

Stabs himself

LODOVICO
  O bloody period!
GRATIANO
  All that's spoke is marr'd.
OTHELLO
  I kiss'd thee ere I kill'd thee: no way but this;
  Killing myself, to die upon a kiss.

Falls on the bed, and dies

CASSIO
  This did I fear, but thought he had no weapon;
  For he was great of heart.
LODOVICO
  [To IAGO] O Spartan dog,
  More fell than anguish, hunger, or the sea!

Look on the tragic loading of this bed;
This is thy work: the object poisons sight;
Let it be hid. Gratiano, keep the house,
And seize upon the fortunes of the Moor,
For they succeed on you. To you, lord governor,
Remains the censure of this hellish villain;
The time, the place, the torture: O, enforce it!
Myself will straight aboard: and to the state
This heavy act with heavy heart relate.

Exeunt

Biography

A Short Life of Edward de Vere,
17th Earl of Oxford

by Dr. Kevin Gilvary, President
The de Vere Society

He was born on 12 April 1550 at Castle Hedingham, his family's ancestral home. His father, John de Vere, 16th Earl, was Lord Great Chamberlain and attended the coronations of both Mary and Elizabeth Tudor. His mother was Margaret Golding. Edward was 11 when, in 1561, Queen Elizabeth visited Hedingham for four days of masques, feasting and entertainments. When his father died in 1562, young Oxford left to become, like Bertram in *All's Well that Ends Well*, a ward of the Crown under the guardianship of William Cecil, the Queen's private secretary (later Lord Burghley, Lord Treasurer). His mother married Charles Tyrrell and seems to have passed out of the boy's life. His sister Mary went to live with her stepfather and the siblings were not reunited for some years.

According to a curriculum in Cecil's own hand, Edward de Vere's daily studies included dancing, French, Latin, writing and drawing, cosmography, penmanship, riding, shooting, exercise and prayer. Edward de Vere showed a prodigious talent for scholarship from his early years, and we may ascribe his lifelong love of learning to the influence of two of his early tutors. The first was Sir Thomas Smith who was, perhaps, England's most respected Greek scholar and the former Cambridge tutor of Sir William Cecil. It was, no doubt, through Cecil's influence that Edward de Vere spent some time living in the household of Smith in his early years, during which time he spent about five months at Smith's alma mater, Queens' College, Cambridge. Smith was a scholar of widely varied interests – this was reflected in his 400-volume library, some of which is still extant at Cambridge. De Vere's other tutor was Laurence Nowell, who was not only an accomplished cartographer but was also England's premier scholar of Anglo-Saxon literature – it was Nowell who possessed the only known copy of *Beowulf*.

Another important influence on Edward de Vere's early studies was his maternal uncle Arthur Golding, an officer in the Court of Wards under Cecil, who is credited with the translation of Ovid's *Metamorphoses*, published in 1567, a book widely recognised as having a major influence on 'Shakespeare'.

Following on from his matriculation at Cambridge in November 1558, Edward was awarded an honorary MA by Cambridge during a Royal progress in August 1564, and another degree by Oxford University during a Royal progress in 1566. Edward de Vere then attended Gray's Inn to study law. One notable feature of the Elizabethan Inns of Court was a tradition of mounting dramatic productions and of hosting the various touring companies of players.

In 1570 he served in a military campaign in Scotland under the Earl of Sussex. By 1571, he was reported as a leading luminary of the Court and, for a time, a favourite of Queen Elizabeth. In December 1571 he married Anne Cecil, aged 15, daughter of his guardian. This was a dynastic marriage where all the advantage accrued to Cecil who, ennobled as Baron Burghley, had reduced the social gap between himself and the young Earl.

While Oxford was away on a Grand Tour of Europe, he heard that his daughter Elizabeth Vere had been born in July 1575. On his return in early 1576, he appeared to have been convinced that Elizabeth was not his child; consequently he became estranged from Anne for five years, and exiled himself from Court, taking up residence in the Savoy and concerning himself with literary and musical patronage.

Already, in 1573, *Cardanus Comfort* (the Consolations of Boethius) had been translated from Latin by Thomas Bedingfield and dedicated to Oxford; and published with a preface written by him. In 1576 an anthology, *A Paradise of Daintie Devices*, including several poems by Oxford, was published. These are juvenile works but already show affinities, in both style and thought, with those of the mature Shakespeare.

Oxford's Grand Tour had taken in Paris, Strasbourg, Venice, Genoa, Florence, Palermo and, on his way back through France, Rousillon – the setting for *Love's Labour's Lost*. Oxford spent the best part of a year travelling in Italy in 1576, and becoming involved with moneylenders. He came back to England fluent in Italian and well acquainted with the northern Italian cities, to be satirised by Gabriel Harvey as 'The Italian Earl'. On his way back his ship was attacked by pirates in the English Channel (cf. *Hamlet*). Fourteen of 'Shakespeare's' plays have Italian settings, in which he put his detailed knowledge of the country, beyond pure book knowledge, to good use.

1573 saw the birth of Henry Wriothesley, Earl of Southampton. Although history has not bequeathed to us any evidence of a direct relationship between the two men, in the relatively small world of the royal Court, they must have been acquainted with each other. The poems *Venus and Adonis* (1593) and *The Rape of Lucrece* (1594) were dedicated to Southampton. These were the first works to be published under the name 'Shakespeare' and for the next five years the records show the byline 'Shakespeare' to have been associated exclusively with these two poems. Plays under the name 'Shakespeare' did not appear in print until 1598, the year that Lord Burghley died.

In May 1577 Oxford invested in Frobisher's voyage in the ship *Edward Bonaventure*. Despite its name, the ship's voyage across the Atlantic in search of the North-West Passage lost money; consequently he was forced to sell three estates (cf. Hamlet's words 'I am but mad north-north-west' II.1.). In 1578 he invested in Frobisher's second expedition, which also lost money, forcing further sales of estates.

He was mentioned by Gabriel Harvey in an address to Queen Elizabeth in July 1578, as a prolific private poet and one 'whose countenance shakes spears'. In the same year John Lyly, Oxford's secretary, published *Euphues.The Anatomy of Wit*, followed in 1579 by *Euphues and his England*, dedicated to Oxford. These two books launched the fashion for 'Euphuism', a style characterized by high-flown language, satirized in *Love's Labour's Lost*.

In March 1581 Oxford's mistress, Anne Vavasour, who was one of Queen Elizabeth's Ladies of the Bedchamber, gave birth to a son. The lovers and their son were sent to the Tower by an infuriated Queen but swiftly released (cf. *Measure for Measure*). After his release, Oxford was wounded in a street-fight provoked by Thomas Knyvet, a kinsman of Anne Vavasour; affrays continued in the streets of London between the rival gangs of supporters for over a year (cf.*Romeo and Juliet*).

In December 1581 he resumed living with his long-suffering and devoted wife, and accepted Elizabeth

Vere as his child. Tragically, their only son died one day after his birth. Three more daughters followed, of whom Susan and Bridget survived.

In 1584, Robert Greene's *Gwydonius; the Card of Fancy* was dedicated to him, identifying him as a 'pre-eminent writer'. In 1586, when he was 36, he served on the tribunal which condemned Mary, Queen of Scots to execution.

In the same year, the Queen awarded Oxford an unconditional pension of £1,000 a year for life (about £500,000 at today's value). The motive for this uncharacteristic generosity on the part of the Queen remains a mystery – no accounting was required of Oxford. Her successor, King James I, continued to pay the pension. In reply to Sir Robert Cecil's request that Lord Sheffield's pension be increased, the King refused, saying, 'Great Oxford got no more . . .', leaving us to wonder why Great Oxford? His greatness does not seem to have resided in war or any of the known offices of State. Perhaps a clue can be found in a letter to Burghley, written in 1594, in which Edward de Vere seeks his favour in a matter involving what he describes as 'in mine office' and that this office is beholden to the Queen.

In 1589, George Puttenham published *The Arte of English Poesie* and this contains the most telling recognition of Edward de Vere's literary standing amongst his contemporaries: 'And in her Majesties time that now is are sprong up an other crew of Courtly makers Noble men and Gentlemen of her Majesties owne servantes, who have written excellently well as it would appeare if their doings could be found out and made publicke with the rest, of which number is first that noble Gentleman Edward Earle of Oxford.'

In 1588 his wife Anne, daughter of Lord Burghley, died and in extant letters written at this time, it is reported that Burghley is so incapacitated by grief over the death of his favourite daughter that he is incapable of conducting any Privy Council business.

Three years later, in 1591, Oxford married another of the Queen's Maids of Honour, Elizabeth Trentham, with whom he finally became the father of a male heir; Henry de Vere, 18th Earl of Oxford. Although there is evidence of his continued involvement in Court affairs, from the date of this marriage Edward de Vere's life at his new home at King's Place in Hackney is perhaps the most obscure of his entire life.

In 1594, his ship the *Edward Bonaventure* was wrecked in Bermuda (cf. *The Tempest*). In January 1595, Elizabeth Vere married William Stanley, 6th Earl of Derby, another literary earl who maintained his own company of players – many scholars believe that *A Midsummer Night's Dream* was written for these festivities which were attended by the whole royal Court.

On September 7 1598, Francis Meres' *Palladis Tamia* was registered for publication, naming Oxford as the 'best for comedy'. This is a vital document in Shakespearean history because it includes the first mention of 'Shakespeare' as a playwright, attributing twelve plays to him; until then Shakespeare's reputation had rested on the two narrative poems only.

Oxford suffered all his life from financial difficulties, much of which can be traced to the fact that Queen Elizabeth handed out the bulk of his estate to her favourite courtier the Earl of Leicester during Oxford's minority as a royal ward (estates which Oxford found almost impossible to reclaim), and the ruinous debt she placed upon him over his marriage to Anne Cecil. It is, however, notable that his new brother-in-law, the wealthy Staffordshire landowner and Knight of the Shire Francis Trentham, took over the management of Edward de

Vere's near-bankrupt estate from 1591 and gradually nursed it back to health so that, when Oxford died, all of his massive debts had been cleared.

On the Queen's death in 1603 Oxford wrote eloquently to Sir Robert Cecil, son and heir of Lord Burghley, of his 'great grief'. He wrote, 'In this common shipwreck, mine is above all the rest, who least regarded, though often comforted, she hath left to try my fortune among the alterations of time and chance'.

Oxford died in Hackney in 1604, cause unknown. Parish records state that he was buried in Hackney Church on July 6, but a family history by his first cousin Percival Golding, states 'Edward de Veer ... a man in mind and body absolutely accomplished with honorable endowments ... lieth buried at Westminster'. No record of such a burial can now be traced in Westminster Abbey, where there is a Vere family tomb.

The Aftermath of Oxford's life and death

During the winter season 1604-05, six of Shakespeare's plays were presented at Court by command of King James I. This has an air of commemoration. In 1609 the *Sonnets* were published in a pirated edition. The famous dedication describes the author as 'our ever-living', a phrase invariably used only of the dead.

In 1622 Henry Peacham published, in *The Compleat Gentelman*, a list of poets who made Elizabeth's reign a 'golden age'. Unaccountably, he omitted Shakespeare but placed the Earl of Oxford in first place in his list – perhaps he knew them to be the same person. This is unlike Meres who included them both – maybe one reason was because he didn't know Oxford and Shakespeare were the same person.

168

We do not know who instigated publication of the First Folio Edition of the Shakespeare plays in 1623, but there is no mention of any executor or relative of Shakspere of Stratford in connection with it. However, of the two brothers who financed it and to whom it was dedicated, one – Philip Earl of Montgomery – was the husband of Oxford's daughter Susan, while the other – William Earl of Pembroke – had once been a suitor for her sister Bridget. Pembroke was Lord Chamberlain, the supreme authority in the world of theatre, and thus in a position to decide which plays were to be published and which suppressed. We also know that Ben Jonson, who wrote much of the introductory material, was an intimate associate of the de Vere family after Oxford's death. The First Folio was therefore very much a family affair, but the family was not the one in Stratford-on-Avon.

An AfterVerse

For those with yet an interest
In strenuous debate
We've compiled a list of books and films
Your appetite to sate.
From this study clear your mind
Of doubt and all misgiving-
Who from us has long since gone
And who is ever-living.

Selected References & Bibliography
About the Author
Edward de Vere, 17th Earl of Oxford

Books

♦ Anderson, M. (2005). *Shakespeare by Another Name: The Life of Edward de Vere, Earl of Oxford, The Man who was Shakespeare.* New York: Gotham Books. *--A physicist by training with research interest in how evidence supports or negates a theory, Mark Anderson spent ten years investigating Edward de Vere as the author of Shake-speare's works.*

♦Farina, William. (2006). *De Vere as Shakespeare: An Oxfordian Reading of the Canon.*
Jefferson, NC. McFarland & Company.

--Each of the plays and poems is individually assessed and explored in its own chapter, using the innumerable connections between the text itself and the life of its author, Edward de Vere.

♦ Looney, J. Thomas (2018). *Shakespeare Identified.* Cary, N.C. Veritas Publicaations.
--First published in 1920 this book began the modern Oxfordian movement. From reading it, Sigmund Freud became convinced and John Galsworthy called it "the best detective story I ever read."

♦ Ogburn, C. (1992). *The Mysterious William Shakespeare.* McLean (Va.): EPM.
--An in depth exploration and must read foundational book on the authorship question.

♦Sobran, Joseph. (1997). *Alias Shakespeare: Solving the Greatest Literary Mystery of All Time.*
New York; The Free Press, A Division of Simon & Schuster.
--A concise exploration of the puzzling questions surrounding the authorship controversy with the evidence decisively supporting the case for Edward de Vere, the 17th Earl of Oxford, as the rightful author of the Shakespeare plays and poems.

♦Whittemore, Hank. (2016), *100 Reasons Shake-speare Was the Earl of Oxford.*
Somerville MA. Forever Press.
► Also with further discussion and public comment at: *Hank Whittemore's Shakespeare Blog.*
        https://hankwhittemore.com/
--In both the book and online blog cited above, Whittemore presents a concise introduction to the

authorship question that examines 100 different aspects, from biographical and historical records, that point to Edward de Vere as the true writer of the Shake-speare plays and poems.

Websites & Videos

► De Vere Society. (2019). The de Vere Society – Dedicated to the proposition that the works of Shakespeare were written by Edward de Vere, 17th Earl of Oxford. [online] Deveresociety.co.uk. Available at: https://deveresociety.co.uk
--A very complete resource with substantial biographical and authorship information and links.

► The Oxford Fellowship (2019). Shakespeare Oxford Fellowship | Research and Discussion of the Shakespeare Authorship Question. [online] Shakespeare Oxford Fellowship. Available at: https://shakespeareoxfordfellowship.org/
--A seminal online resource especially focusing on the authorship question.

► Waugh, A. (2019). Alexander Waugh. [online] YouTube. Available at: https://www.youtube.com/channel/UCHN7SCKlsa9lPYJ mqqQ2uIg/featured/
OR simply search: 'Alexander Waugh'
--Alexander Waugh is a leading authorship scholar who has produced many fascinating video presentations on the authorship question. This link is to his YouTube Channel.

► Columbia Pictures & Centropolis Entertainment. (2011). *Anonymous.* Produced and directed by Roland Emmerich. [DVD]
--*This mainstream film is both entertaining and enlightening. It presents a superb dramatization of the character of Edward de Vere, setting out in detail the historical and personal context which made his anonymous authorship necessary.*

►Centropolis Entertainment and First Folio Pictures. *Last Will and Testament.* (2012). [DVD]
--*A thoughtful and ground-breaking video documentary introduction to the Shakespeare authorship question.*

Acknowledgment
Our sincere thanks to
The de Vere Society
and
The Shakespeare Oxford Fellowship
*for their inspiration, help and support
in creating this series.*

Attributions
*--Character list from Wikipedia under
the Creative Commons License 3.0
--Play text from the Moby(tm) editions
in the public domain*

Photos

Coat of Arms of Edward de Vere
Source: Wikimedia.org
Author: George Baker / Public domain

The Keep at Castle Hedingham
Source: geograph.org.uk
Author: David Phillips / CC BY-SA 2.0

The de Vere Family Coat of Arms
Source: Wikimedia
Author: Rs-nourse / CC BY-SA 3.0
(https://creativecommons.org/licenses/by-sa/3.0)

View from The Minstrels' Gallery, Hedingham Castle
Source: geograph.org.uk/p/3162585
Photo by: © PAUL FARMER - cc-by-sa/2.0

Cover/Inside: The Welbeck portrait of Edward de Vere (1575).
Artist unknown. National Portrait Gallery, London.

This work has been edited and produced by

Verus Publishing
www.verusbooks.com

V | P

www.ingramcontent.com/pod-product-compliance
Lightning Source LLC
Chambersburg PA
CBHW030417100426
42812CB00028B/3000/J